the conductor's workshop

A WORKBOOK ON INSTRUMENTAL CONDUCTING

R. Gerry Long

WM. C. BROWN COMPANY PUBLISHERS
Dubuque, Iowa

MUSIC SERIES

Consulting Editor
Frederick W. Westphal
Sacramento State College

Fifth Printing, 1975

Printed in the United States of America

TO TETA,
JOFF AND DIDI

Contents

Preface

The Conductor's Workshop, a workbook for the beginning conducting class, is written for the student who desires not only to develop a secure baton technique, but who wishes also to learn in the conducting class how to apply that baton technique in attaining high musical standards. The twofold purpose of the workbook is first, to provide musical materials for a small ensemble so that such an ensemble can be available to the student in the conducting class, and second, to provide a teaching technique geared to the use of such materials, emphasizing the solution to fundamental musical problems which confront all conductors.

Having experienced the conducting class both as student and teacher, and the orchestra as player and conductor, it is my feeling that our music schools most frequently cannot provide the practical experience which is necessary in the training of conductors. This is due primarily to the inaccessability of the school orchestra, the lack of usable conducting drill materials for a smaller ensemble, and the absence of an approach which is designed for a class in which a small ensemble is used, and in which the students have frequent opportunity to experience the everyday musical problems which all conductors experience. It would be futile to assemble a small group of instrumentalists for which little usable music exists. Most music schools depend on the availability—however rare—of the school ensembles —band or orchestra. In my own undergraduate training, for example, my band conducting course afforded only one opportunity to conduct a university ensemble, and my orchestral conducting course afforded no such opportunity. This is not an unusual situation, and the problem becomes more acute as our music schools increase in size. I concluded that this problem could be solved only through the use of original musical examples for a small ensemble of musicians, with specific conducting problems in mind—a type of *Gebrauchsmusik.*

The absence of an approach designed for a class in which students are regularly conducting live musicians results in another serious weakness in conducting class methods currently in use. The hit-and-miss approach to the application of conducting technique—one day conducting a pianist, the next day in front of a mirror, the next day a recorded orchestra, and one day in front of the university orchestra—results in the inability of the student to get beyond baton techniques and into the musical problems of an ensemble. Therefore, most students coming from our music schools have some baton technique which they have had no opportunity to adequately test in front of musicians, and they have not been tested at all as to their ability to produce musical results with an ensemble of musicians. "Getting through" the assigned piece becomes the overwhelming goal. Making music frequently is not even considered.

Furthermore, the organization of nearly all of the textbooks on the art of conducting is such that these texts do not consider in detail the fundamental musical obstacles, other than that of baton technique, which might contribute to the failure of a young conductor. The problem of tuning the orchestra, for example, is usually either completely ignored, or at best, given one or two pages.

The approach taken in this workbook is that of stressing baton technique, applying baton technique in front of performing musicians, and also emphasizing those ensemble fundamentals which a conductor must control in order to guide an orchestra to an accurate, convincing and expressive interpretation. If the conducting student is not made aware of the urgency of extracting the best possible musical results from his fellow students, he may set a pattern which makes him forever incapable of accomplishing this task with any performing group.

This book does not attempt to deal with the many extramusical traits which are a part of a successful conductor (i. e., organizational ability, personality, leadership ability, public relations expertise, etc.). Nor does it attempt to be a musical lexicon for the conductor, with sample programs, summaries of musical forms, dictionary of musical terms, seating charts, etc. It attempts only to fill the void—the lack of original material for the small ensemble which can serve the conducting student in class —which presently exists.

My deepest gratitude is extended to a number of musicians whose generous assistance helped to make this book possible. They are Dr. Norman Hunt and Dr. Frederick Westphal of Sacramento State College, Dr. Glenn R. Williams and Professor Ralph G. Laycock of Brigham Young University, Dr. Vernon B. Read of San Jose State College, and Mr. Norman Carol, concertmaster of the Philadelphia Orchestra. To Mr. Carol's colleague in the orchestra, Mr. John De Lancie, principal oboist, who gave many hours of his time in providing the perspective of a musician who has played under virtually every great conductor of the past twenty-five years, I owe a special debt of gratitude. I wish also to express my thanks to Mrs. Irene Gallagher for her assistance in typing—ever so patiently— the manuscript.

R. GERRY LONG

Introduction

CONDUCTING "LIVE" MUSICIANS

The most obvious way to learn to conduct a musical ensemble such as an orchestra, or a band, is to practice conducting live musicians. Conducting a recording, a pianist, or one's mirror image, though somewhat helpful, is not adequate. Usually the large ensemble—orchestra or band—is not available to the student for practice. Most often in a conducting class when a student is finally given his long-awaited opportunity in front of the university orchestra, he is petrified. Why? Because he has never had an opportunity to try out even such a simple gesture as the downbeat with an ensemble, to say nothing of his crescendo, his cut-off, his cuing, and all other simple gestures which can become immense problems when used all-at-once in a work of relative difficulty such as a Beethoven overture.

When the downbeat is introduced in class, each student should be able to try out that gesture with live musicians—even though only two or three musicians may be available. The same is true for the introduction of all other new gestures. In this way, the student's initial conducting experience with an orchestral composition might well be his twentieth time on the podium. Present conducting training programs, in which an orchestra is seldom available, are inadequate. A small ensemble of live musicians must serve as a substitute.

Many of the problems of conducting such a small ensemble are the same as those problems encountered in conducting an orchestra or a band. (Since the wind band [*Blaskapelle* or *Blasorchester* in German] is an orchestra without strings, the term "orchestra" will refer to a wind band as well as the traditional orchestra with strings.)

The use of a special small ensemble is very rare because of the absence of musical materials for such a group. Max Rudolf, in his book, *The Grammar of Conducting*, includes some conducting examples which he has composed for piano. He recommends that they be arranged for a small orchestra, though I know of no conducting class which has actually done the arrangements. Such literature should present the type of problems which would offer a challenge to the young conductor, while at the same time not requiring virtuoso chamber musicians to perform the music. A Haydn quartet movement, for example, would be—for the student conductor's purposes—too easy to conduct, and too difficult to perform.

Contained in this workbook are over two hundred original examples of music for small ensembles which are easy to perform, but challenging to conduct.

EXPERIENCING REAL PROBLEMS

Naturally an orchestra (or band) would serve the purpose of a student conductor most adequately. But since these groups are rarely available, the student must find an alternative experience. The conductor must somehow experience—and be guided in the solution to—such problems as a poor attack, a missed entrance, the confusion created when he conducts three-four instead of four-four time, and an ensemble which drags or rushes the tempo. He must also experience wrong notes, poor intonation, lack of dynamic contrast, questionable tone quality, ragged rhythmic ensemble, and insensitive interpretation. All of these problems of ensemble musicianship can be observed and corrected in a small ensemble, exactly as they must be observed and corrected in a full orchestra. If a conductor does not recognize weak ensemble playing in a trio, he will not recognize it later in a full orchestra.

Each of the examples in the workbook has been composed to stress a specific conducting problem. They have all been composed with emphasis on technical simplicity, so that they may be played by almost any three instrumentalists having the performance proficiency of the average college sophomore. For this reason the conducting examples utilize simple keys and technically uncomplicated melodic patterns. Another reason for using such simple melodic materials in the musical examples is to free the student conductor to begin his conducting experience with concentration on extremely simple musical fundamentals (i. e., a triad played well in tune by three instruments, quarter notes and eighth notes fitting together perfectly, clean articulation or bowing, etc.). There is no point in moving on to an overture until the student proves himself capable of attaining these fundamentals with an instrumental trio.

ORGANIZATION OF THE CONDUCTING "TEAM"

The musical examples composed for the conducting class call for a specific physical set-up for a group or groups of four students, with three students performing while one conducts. If the class is larger, two or more "teams" of students may work in groups of four. If there are one, two or three extra students, they can be added to one or more teams of four to alternate with the other students and to observe and criticize. The music is written for many combinations of instruments—using treble, tenor and bass parts (i. e., clarinet, alto sax, and trombone; or violin, viola and bassoon). All parts are written in concert pitch, necessitating transposition by non-concert pitch instruments. Since most conducting classes are offered in the junior or senior years, instrumentalists will have generally reached a level where transposition will not be a major problem, or their proficiency in a minor instrument will have developed to a degree which will enable them to change instruments for a class rather than to transpose. (A violist might play cello in the class.)

TWO PRIMARY OBJECTIVES

The immediate purpose of this approach to conducting, as suggested in the preface, is to provide an ensemble of live musicians with which to apply and test the student conductor's technique. Perhaps even more important than a test of the conductor's technique though, is the opportunity for the teacher to observe the conducting student in each class period under actual conducting conditions. Only in the presence of a live performing group will the teacher be able to observe the student's reaction to shoddy execution of musical fundamentals after the student has developed some security in his baton technique. In other words, the student should not only conduct well, he should demand from the ensemble the highest level of performance.

It is the conducting teacher's responsibility to make the student aware of musical fundamentals such as tone, intonation, articulation, bowing, balance, rhythmic ensemble, and interpretation, and to see that he pursues the proper execution of these fundamentals with his every conducting gesture and comment.

DEMANDING MUSICAL RESULTS

The student conductor's ability to extract from the other musicians not just an execution of the conducting exercise, but a *performance* of the highest level in regards to all musical details (tone, intonation, rhythmic ensemble, articulation, bowing, balance, and interpretation) will depend on a variety of factors. Certain of these factors, such as the student's personality, his personal relationships with the members of the ensemble, his organizational ability, etc., are outside the province of this workbook.

However, the most important factor which influences the conductor's ability to obtain good musical results from his musicians is his own musicianship. This should be the *prime* concern of both the student conductor and the teacher. For if the student should complete the conducting course with a superb baton technique, and in the process of learning such a technique, he should not develop high standards of ensemble performance, half of the value of having had live musicians present will have been lost. And what the teacher can expect the student conductor to extract from the ensemble cannot exceed the student's own musicianship. The quality of performance of an ensemble is very much a mirror of the musical thinking of the conductor of the ensemble.

ASPECTS OF MUSICIANSHIP—FUNDAMENTALS

The approach taken in this workbook to the development of musicianship is based on my own breakdown of general musicianship for the conductor into isolated fundamentals or concepts already listed above as tone, intonation, rhythmic ensemble, articulation, bowing, balance and inter-pretation. Another important fundamental, that of technical accuracy, (playing the correct note—e. g., D♯ as opposed to D), will not be included, as it is too obvious, and, of all of the fundamentals, perhaps the least overlooked. And if the conductor cannot begin by demanding the notes as printed in the score, there is no point in considering such "complexities" as intonation and interpretation.

The fundamental concepts which will be stressed are listed in an order which is based on my own personal preference. The order is of little importance anyway, as long as all of the fundamentals are eventually covered. I feel most inclined to begin with tone, then intonation, without which no musical performance can sound satisfactory.

When tone and intonation are highly polished, there has been established in the orchestra a concrete foundation which can enhance the execution of such fundamentals as rhythmic ensemble, articulation and balance. Interpretation is mentioned last not for reason of its lack of importance, but because it is a combination of all musical fundamentals well executed and more, and it must be sought at every moment in a rehearsal.

Until a conductor has developed in his "inner ear" a concept of these fundamentals—good tone, intonation, etc.,—he will be unable to demand from an orchestra a musical execution of these fundamentals, and conse-quently, of any complete composition.

THE ROLE OF BASIC MUSICIANSHIP

A successful conductor must first be a good musician. Whether or not this sounds naive or cynical, there can be no doubt that there are many unmusical conductors who have the courage to step onto a podium. Con-sider, on the other hand, the musical capabilities of great conductors, past and present, in their non-conducting rolls: Mitropoulis, Szell, Bernstein, all excellent pianists; Ormandy, violinist; Katims, violist; Toscanini, cel-list; Koussevitzky, bassist; Colin Davis, clarinetist, etc. A conductor who has not experienced the problems involved in making music with other musicians (intonation, balance, tone quality, articulation, rhythmic ensem-ble, interpretation, etc.), will not have the experience to draw upon when he has to guide four horn players in tuning a diminished seventh chord, when he must extract more soulful playing from the solo oboist in Strauss' *Don Juan*, when the woodwinds sound muddy in Mendelssohn's *Midsum-mernight's Dream* Scherzo, or when the cello and viola sections do not blend in Brahm's *Haydn Variations*.

It is true that one occasionally meets a rather successful conductor who has not been a virtuoso performer. This is a rare musician who has exceptional insight regarding the performance of music. His lack of experi-ence on an instrument is frequently replaced by an insatiable curiosity about performance from the standpoint of pedagogical understanding. In this case, his substitute for a personal performing experience is an *excep-tionally* well-trained ear, which is developed through endless listening experiences. An eminently successful conductor of a college concert band,

and a non-performer, never misses the Metropolitan Opera performances in Detroit even if he must use standing-room-only tickets. Through a lifetime of this type of concert going he has developed unusually fine concepts of performance which he passes on to his musicians.

But for every one such musician who has developed his musicianship in spite of the lack of a personal performing experience, there are dozens of non-performers who are not correcting shortcomings in their musical training. Often the priceless benefits which come to the perceptive listener are also missed. MANY CONDUCTORS, PARTICULARLY IN MUSIC EDUCATION, DO NOT CARE TO ATTEND CONCERTS OR LISTEN TO SERIOUS RECORDED MUSIC. It certainly seems impossible that a non-performer could ever become a successful conductor if he were also not an avid concert-goer and/or record enthusiast.

PART I

CONCEPTS
AND
FUNDEMENTALS

CONCEPTS AND FUNDAMENTALS

The key word in a conductor's development should be "concept." Without an orchestra in front of him, what can the conductor conceive or picture in his inner ear at the mention of such things, for example, as good trombone tone, a major-minor seventh chord (in tune), woodwind articulation, the brass passages of Siegfried's funeral music in Wagner's *Götterdämmerung*, a cymbal crash (not just careless banging of two cymbals together), rubato in an ascending and descending arpeggio, the exciting sound of a string quartet playing a ff tremolo, or even the sound of a single violinist drawing forth maximum tone from a single half note? All of these, plus thousands of other more elaborate musical pictures must be conceived in the conductor's ear, and made real by him through his orchestra.

1

The sound produced by a given orchestra will lean towards the sound which is anticipated by the conductor. What the conductor wants to hear—the conductor's concept—should eventually come from the orchestra. Most weak orchestras are the products of conductors who have vague concepts, or who cannot get a good concept across to the orchestra. Of course, there are limitations in what a conductor should expect within each orchestral proficiency level. A conductor should not expect a high school orchestra with three amateur string basses to sound like a major symphony with ten professional string basses. But the same high school orchestra should be approached with the intent that it will sound like the *best* high school orchestra. So it is that the Denver Symphony, for example, while not attempting to imitate the Philadelphia Orchestra, should strive for such lofty concepts of pitch, tone, etc., as one finds in the Philadelphia orchestra.

DEVELOPING CONCEPTS

The development of such concepts requires a life-long involvement with ensemble performance. Students occasionally seek advice on majoring in conducting. My first advice is: become as proficient as possible on a major instrument and the piano. Through proficiency on the viola or oboe, for example, a student will experience the problems of expressing music individually, and through increased proficiency, he will be taken into better ensemble groups, to experience a higher calibre of ensemble performance. One eminent conductor suggests that no one should become a conductor until he has exhausted the expressive possibilities of his own instrument.

A young musician who can serve effectively as player-coach for a string quartet, woodwind quintet, or brass ensemble, has completed a number of the rudimentary steps to becoming a good conductor. In the process he has either developed good concepts of tone, intonation, articulation, bowing, balance, rhythmic precision, and expression, or he has applied the concepts after having learned them from other experiences, such as private teachers, other conductors, or endless listening to live and recorded music.

A concept of the proper execution of each of the fundamentals—tone, intonation, articulation, bowing, balance, rhythmic ensemble, and interpretation—must be pursued by the conductor relentlessly. An orchestra which has overlooked the fundamentals of tone, intonation, balance, and phrasing, and cannot sight-read a chorale beautifully may never play it beautifully, since the performance of that chorale demands simply a musically sound execution of those musical fundamentals in a simple composition. A conductor who does not have a highly developed concept of these musical fundamentals will never produce a thoroughly musical organization whether his group be a high school orchestra or the Berlin Philharmonic.

> Only a man . . . whose conception of the work does not dwarf it, and who is capable of lifting his medium up to the level of that work is worthy of the name of conductor.[1]

PIANO BACKGROUND

All of the great conductors who have taught conducting recommend a background in piano, which must include transposition and the reading of unusual clefs such as alto and tenor. A conductor with keyboard facility will not only be better able to find out what is contained in an unfamiliar score, but he will be better able to "think harmonically." Musicians who have played a single line instrument are not as likely to be able to imagine a progression of chords without hearing it played. Pianists are less likely to hear a composition as a combination of melodies for

1. Herman Scherchen, *Handbook of Conducting* (London: Oxford University Press, 1933), p. 3.

different instruments, but rather as a vertical structure. In keeping with the idea of developing concepts, a harmonic concept can best be developed through knowledge of a harmonic, (i.e., a keyboard), instrument. The aspiring conductor should train his "inner ear"—his musical imagination—so that he can look at a simple chord progression and hear the harmony without the aid of a piano. The piano background will aid in developing this ability to imagine a sound before hearing it. The conductor must be able to imagine the sound of full chords, the sound of two or more melodies being played simultaneously, and the sound of the rhythmic sweep of the music. A capable conductor can encounter an unfamiliar work from the Viennese Classical period, for example, and learn the entire work—developing an accurate aural picture of the work—without hearing an orchestral performance or playing a piano reduction of the work.

The student who develops an interest in conducting without having had adequate piano experience must develop enough piano technique and reading ability to at least play slowly through an orchestra score. Many conductors shy away from contemporary works after attempting them with their orchestra because they cannot hear the sonorities which the composer intended. With a piano it is possible to take the time to analyze each unusual sonority—to dissect it—to relate it to traditional sonorities—in short, to understand the sonority so that he can enlighten his musicians as he exposes them to a new work, rather than entering into it as he would enter a dark and unfamiliar forest. The conductor must guide the orchestra into new worlds of sound but he must first know the terrain.

ORCHESTRAL FUNDAMENTALS

We have earlier expressed the belief that highly developed musical concepts of orchestral fundamentals can best be achieved through artistic accomplishment on an instrument. However, there are certain means for improving such concepts for those who have not had an extensive background on an instrument, and for those who are interested in a broader approach to developing musicianship. Part One of this workbook contains suggested steps for pursuing such improved concepts. It is suggested that each student read these chapters thoroughly, and that they be discussed in the conducting class before and during the involvement with the conducting examples of chapters seven through thirteen.

All of the fundamentals of orchestral performance discussed in the following chapters are important to the conductor who is preparing himself to conduct an orchestra. Some conductors have consummate knowledge of baton technique and orchestral repertory, but are lacking in knowledge of basic orchestral fundamentals. Many of these conductors are aware of their weaknesses and are taking the necessary steps to correct them. Others, however, remain frustrated by the problems within their orchestra which they cannot solve because they do not have the technical knowledge to solve the problems.

THE NEED FOR ADEQUATE PREPARATION

Their dilemma is that although there may be a number of professionally qualified musicians in their orchestras, they themselves are not equipped to help the non-professional to develop towards professionalism. A conductor cannot simply resign himself, for example, to the harsh sound of an oboist just because the oboist is a lawyer by profession, or an elementary school band director, or a college sophomore. We cannot expect that every conductor will know how to make a more pleasant sounding oboe reed, but he should know that a different oboe reed will produce a different sound, and that a stiff reed is the cause of the harshness and the inability to attack with control, and that a reed which is too soft may cause an uncontrolled pitch. The conductor of a semi-professional orchestra must know these details. Should not conductors of fully professional orchestras also be expected to know them? Or are we allowing too many conductors to "guide" major orchestras without first having proven their competence with a semi-professional orchestra?

To expect a conductor to take the time to find a solution to such problems is to expect absolute professionalism from him. Absolute professionalism requires a great commitment of time— time to learn fundamentals, time to study scores, time to continue to improve one's own instrumental ability, time to read and develop one's artistic and aesthetic tastes, time to compose and to orchestrate, time to listen perceptively, and time to think.

Many conductors accept too many obligations and do not have the time to prepare themselves adequately for each concert. A young conductor might endanger his entire professional career by accepting engagements without time to prepare them. Above all, the conductor must allow himself time to become familiar with every detail of the score. He must study each work until he is acquainted with each melody, each countermelody, each accompanying figure, each rhythm, each chordal sonority, etc. He must sing every voice in order to know in advance any unusual problems which will occur. He must sing each voice while imagining other voices in relation to the one he is singing. He must anticipate and plan a solution for each problem which will arise.

He must know each work, not only from the standpoint of all of its inner detail—its microcosmic nature—but also from the standpoint of its macrocosmic nature—it relation to the composer's other works, the period which it represents, the philosophical ideas of that period, other aesthetic trends of the time in art, theatre, literature, etc. He must above all understand the architectural structure of the work—the form. If an architect were assigned to reconstruct such a structure as the Parthenon, or a similar structure, he would have to make an exhaustive study of the function of each part in relation to the whole. If a theatrical director wishes to stage *Hamlet*, he must do likewise—study the function of each part in relation to the whole. The conductor's task is like that of the theatre director, to recreate each work he conducts with the utmost understanding of the composer's intent. He must therefore know the architecture, or the form of the work.

Certainly his own musicianship will influence the composition's final shape, but the basic design has been established by the composer. The conductor must arrive at his concept of this design through devoted study and preparation in advance of the first rehearsal. Even a finely trained musician who has not prepared adequately before a rehearsal faces a loss of respect from his musicians.

If a conductor always allows himself time to prepare each program so that it will equal or surpass the artistic level of his previous program, he will continue to grow because he will force a constant re-examination and improvement of his concepts.

Let it be understood that the art of conducting, like the art of becoming a fine human being, is a never-ending search. No one has ever perfected the art, though several have developed it to an inspiring degree. No conductor has been all things to all musicians or to his audience. Every conductor has his weaknesses. Therefore each conductor must, in his own way, strive to progress as a musician throughout his life. It is the hope of the author that this workbook will aid some young conductors in the lifetime quest to conduct effectively—to be truthful to the art.

ORCHESTRAL FUNDAMENTALS AND INTERPRETATION

We have stated that one of the two main objectives of this approach to the study of conducting is to instill in the student an awareness of the basic musical problems (fundamentals) which confront the conductor. These problems or fundamentals already listed and discussed as tone, intonation, rhythmic ensemble, articulation, bowing, balance and interpretation, must be conceived and approached individually, because if any one of them is overlooked in training an ensemble, the overall musical results cannot be satisfactory. If, however, through intelligent and vigorous effort the conductor can achieve a high degree of mastery of each of these six fundamentals, the musical results thus obtained cannot easily be criticized.

The following chapters are devoted to methods of approaching all but the last of these fundamentals, that of interpretation. Interpretation is omitted because, as was pointed out in the introduction, interpretation is the sum of all other fundamentals, plus much more. A workbook of this sort is not the means through which interpretation can be taught. At best we could list some general concepts of rubato, dynamic contrasts, bowings, tempo, etc. and some philosophical ideas on the subject.

A musician's concept of interpretation is dependent on many and varied factors, such as his proficiency on his own instrument, his experience as a listener, his general perception, his innate talent, his life experiences, which effect his philosophy and aesthetic judgment, his ambition, and his emotional make-up, etc. Perhaps one of the most interesting studies of interpretation is to be found in recorded music. One can compare, for example, two performances—one conducted by Serge Koussevitzky, the other by Leopold Stokowski—of the third movement, *Poco allegretto*, of Brahms' *Third Symphony* in F minor, Op. 90. Here one can find two extremes in such important matters of interpretation as tempo, use of rubato, and balance between solo voice and accompanying instruments. The contrasts are quite remarkable.

The other five fundamentals are more concrete, tangible fundamentals. They are technical, rather than aesthetic, and can more easily be controlled. Our objectives in considering each one individually are 1) to make the student more aware of each fundamental as a potential obstacle to good orchestral playing, 2) to develop an improved concept of the best execution of that fundamental, and 3) to suggest means through which the student can find solutions to the problems which relate to that fundamental.

PREREQUISITES FOR THE CONDUCTING CLASS

The conducting class which makes use of this workbook should be so scheduled in the music curriculum as to insure that each entering student will have at least the minimum essential musical background. This should include, in addition to a sufficient skill on an instrument (a voice student should have adequate piano facility), a well developed rhythmic, melodic, and harmonic skill. The following music courses should be offered as prerequisites for the conducting course, if possible:

1. **Harmony:** two years or more; knowledge of traditional intervals, triadic harmony, including 9ths and 11th chords, non-harmonic devices; some knowledge of more contemporary concepts of harmony (e.g. quartal harmony, serial harmony, polytonality, etc.).
2. **Ear training:** aural familiarity and understanding of the above listed materials; sight-singing ability including facility with tenor and alto clefs; considerable rhythmic skill; competence in reading the examples listed in chapter eight, pages 60-62, without serious difficulty.
3. **Keyboard:** at least two years for the music student whose major instrument is not piano.
4. **Music history:** at least an introductory course, but as much additional history as possible. Courses with period specialization (i.e., Baroque, Romantic, Viennese Classical, Impressionism, Serial, etc.).
5. **Acoustics:** knowledge of the harmonic series as applied to a) tone quality of individual instruments, b) relationship of string or air column lengths to the basic intervals and their mathematical ratios; basic knowledge of the physics of sound transfer; rudimentary knowledge of the principal of equal temperament and of pure intervals; acoustical structure of stringed instruments, wind pipes, percussion instruments, etc.
6. **Orchestration:** at least an introductory course.
7. **Instrumental methods:** as many of the required instrumental methods classes as possible, including voice or choral participation.

Chapter 1

Tone

PERCEPTIVE EXPOSURE

To state that tonal concepts are a matter of exposure seems to be an oversimplification. The term "perceptive exposure" might be a more accurate term. To illustrate, conductor 'X', who "played for seventeen years with Toscanini," does not stress the development of ensemble tone in his orchestra. One might assume that seventeen years of exposure to the world's finest musicians would almost guarantee a fine tonal concept. Not so. Conductor 'Y', who was born and raised and went to music school in a small town, extracts from his orchestra a better sound than does conductor 'X'. This is a rare comparison, but such situations do exist. Conductor 'Y' is more perceptive in his listening habits, and realizes the sound which can be produced by each instrument, and the total sound possible by his orchestra. He has made better use of his more limited exposure to quality performance, and that quality has become his concept of tone through *perceptive* exposure. Exposure alone does not produce fine concepts.

DEVELOPING INSTRUMENTAL CURIOSITY

To develop an improved concept of orchestral tone, the conductor must avail himself of every opportunity for exposure to all instruments of the orchestra. If he is a violinist, he will probably have a fine concept of violin tone, and a good concept of string tone in general, but he must make a diligent effort to hear brass ensembles, woodwind quintets, cello, percussion, and flute recitals, jazz bands, community orchestras, high school bands, etc., in order to develop a fine concept of each instrument. He must talk with wind players to learn about wind vibrato, about double reed adjustment, about brass mouthpieces, and the tuba player's selection of CC tuba as opposed to F tuba. The same advice applies to all conductors as they seek to increase their knowledge of instruments other than their own.

One of the best opportunities for the improvement of tonal concepts (as was earlier recommended in studying interpretation) is the comparison of different recorded performances. All of the great orchestras and soloists of the world are recorded today. One's concept of violin tone and interpretation certainly must improve by hearing recordings of Oistrakh, Menuhin, Millstein, Heifetz, Stern and Szeryng playing the Beethoven Concerto in D.

I was personally very much influenced in my concept of trumpet sound when I first heard Harry Glanz's recording of Copland's *Quiet City*. A valuable outside assignment for students in a conducting class is to find contrasting concepts of tone as produced by various solo members of major orchestras. The many recordings of Ravel's Bolero, because of the abundance of solo passages, give fine examples of the sound of the first chair wind players of each orchestra, and an opportunity for the listener to compare one concept of tone with another.

The conductor should develop his awareness of instrumental tone until he is aware not only of the general character of tone on the instrument, but also of various qualities of sound such as bright, dark, heavy, mellow or strident, etc. Awareness of vibrato speed and vibrato amplitude are important. If the conductor is with an orchestra which can select its personnel from many applicants, he can select the type of sound which will best fit his concept of orchestral tone. A conductor at any level (not guest conductors, but regular conductors who train their orchestras) will produce an orchestral sound no better than his own concept of the tone quality of each instrument and of the composite sound of all of the instruments as conceived in his own musical imagination (inner ear). Or, stated more simply, the sound of an orchestra cannot surpass the musical concepts of its conductor.

The influence on an orchestra of a conductor such as Eugene Ormandy or George Szell should be carefully considered in this regard. Mr. Ormandy has now personally appointed almost every member of the Philadelphia Orchestra. What did he have in mind as he selected each individual player? The Philadelphia "string sound" is almost a household word; the Philadelphia brass section is in the opinion of many one of the most homogeneous of sections to be heard. And the woodwind section is built around one of the finest woodwind quintets.

But what of the conductor who cannot select from fifty or more of the best musicians for each vacancy? Again, the matter of individual concept is just as important. In the community or school orchestra, the conductor must gradually improve the sound of his orchestra by imparting improved concepts to his players. This is happening at every level of orchestral playing where a sensitive conductor is in charge—where the conductor is imposing a high standard of performance on his orchestra.

ACOUSTICAL ASPECTS OF TONE

It is advisable that the conductor take an interest in the acoustical aspects of tone; that is, the way in which the acoustical properties of each orchestral instrument effect the relative prominence of certain overtones to give the instrument its special color. One could overestimate the importance of such exposure to the acoustical properties of tone. We would not, for instance, base our selection of a principal horn player on the "appearance" of his tone on an oscilloscope. The purpose of such a study, however, is to provide another approach to the study of tone. It is not the only way or the best way. It can at best provide another perspective on an aspect of instrumental playing which is somewhat abstract and certainly very elusive to many musicians. Every approach to the study of tone can be of help, and while nothing can replace the experience of endless hours of aural involvement with instrumental timbre through playing the instruments, attending recitals, listening to records, living next door to a cellist, etc., a visual experience can add another dimension to the musician's understanding of tone. The conductor must sense that the greatest technical and expressive performance is severely damaged by an undesirable tone, and that every approach to developing a familiarity with instrumental tone color is valuable.

SCHOOL ORCHESTRA CONDUCTORS AND ORCHESTRAL TONE

It is particularly important that a school orchestra director have a highly developed concept of the tone of all of the orchestral instruments. Rarely will the conductor of a high school orchestra have but a few—at best—students interested and dedicated enough to seek professional standards of tone on their instrument. For the most part, the conductor must provide a clear concept of tone for all the orchestral instruments. He must immediately be aware, for example, if his second violins are producing an anemic sound, and he must know the sound that they should be capable of producing at their age level, and how that sound can be produced. The same is true with the tone quality of brass, woodwind and percussion instruments.

The student cannot naturally know what should be a fine tone for his ability-level on his instrument unless he has an excellent private teacher, or unless the conductor creates such a concept by guiding his listening experiences, continually admonishing him to try to improve his tone, taking him to concerts, seeing that he has the finest instruction, etc.

It is not unusual to have a student say that he played the bassoon for three years before he heard a professional player, and only then realized that the constricted, high-pitched tone which he had produced was not characteristic for the instrument.

It is true that a conductor cannot, through some magic formula, simply extract immediately any lofty concept of orchestral tone—of one instrument or of the entire orchestra—which he might desire. However, it happens much too frequently that the musicians could, and would, produce a better sound if the conductor were to make it clear that a much better sound is possible for them.

Chapter 2

Intonation

No fundamental problem facing the conductor poses a greater pitfall than that of tuning. When intonation is erratic in an orchestra, it is difficult to make any aspect of performance convincing. Perhaps the greatest damage done by such intonation, other than its own offensiveness, is the negative effect it has on orchestral tone. In order to achieve good tone quality in an orchestra, it is necessary that the acoustical fundamental tones of two notes be in tune, in order that the overtones of those fundamentals also be in tune. And since it is the overtones which determine the character of sound of an instrument, out-of-tune overtones do not blend, and the ensuing results are displeasing. Beauty of tone is thus impaired by poor intonation.

In addition, ensemble and articulation are obscured by faulty intonation, balance becomes a more serious problem, and interpretation a great frustration. One out-of-tune wind player in a professional section can undermine the spirit of an entire section of pitch-conscious players until they lose their desire to perform in that section.

Curiously, some conductors who possess otherwise strong musical qualifications in other fundamental areas (tone, rhythm, interpretation) are rather indifferent to tuning problems, and they assume that the musicians will work out their own tuning differences. It rarely turns out that way in such an orchestra, and there is a general lack of clarity because of the faulty intonation.

Tuning is such a complex problem that it plagues major symphony orchestras as well as junior high school bands. Although the problem has been a major orchestral frustration throughout the orchestra's history, our highly developed technology of today—influencing instrument construction and providing electronic tuning devices—has made it possible to eliminate at least the most serious problems of tuning an ensemble. However, unless the conductor provides the leadership which encourages individual players to use whatever means are available to improve their intonation concepts, the orchestra will not sound "clean." Again, the orchestra reflects the *conductor's concept* —this time of pitch.

Deficiencies of intonation such as impure octaves, a melodic line in which the woodwinds are out of tune on just two or three notes, a brass crescendo which becomes increasingly sharp, chromatic chordal relationships which require greater accuracy on the part of string players, a trumpet sustaining a slightly sharp, low concert C, and a major triad with the fifth played sharply, must be the conductor's alarm signals. He must immediately stop and correct any such deficiency before continuing. Too often the conductor overlooks such problems because he is not disturbed by them. An orchestral player who is conditioned to expect to be stopped for such intonation errors will eventually begin to correct the problems himself.

Of course it should be understood that not all problems can be corrected in one rehearsal. However, if the conductor makes it known that faulty intonation is an ever-present evil spectre, he can make it one of his major points of emphasis in each rehearsal, and this type of effort will gradually wear away the rough edges of pitch. A conductor who does not stress intonation in each rehearsal is like the carpenter who strikes the nail so carelessly that he leaves hammer marks in the finished woodwork. True, his cabinet might be still functional when finished, but the pitifully poor craftsmanship destroys the beauty of his product.

REHEARSING INTONATION

Every orchestra should begin each rehearsal by playing something which is not too technically involved, such as a chorale-like movement. Each chord and each unison should be perfectly tuned in the process. Through this, intonation can be stressed at each rehearsal without concern for technical problems, with the players devoting nearly all of their attention to intonation. The orchestra can then produce its very best intonation *at least once* in each rehearsal. This will assist the development of improved intonation concepts among both the conductor and his musicians.

With a very young orchestra, certain pitch problems can never be completely eliminated, but no conductor should avoid a sustained effort to eliminate them all. Particularly with a younger orchestra, the problem will have to be approached firmly, but not so incessantly that the players lose their interest through a lack of opportunity to get enough involved in performance.

Almost all musicians will respond positively to a conductor who is pitch-sensitive and who is making an improvement in the orchestra through this sensitivity. The degree of tact and pacing which he uses in his attempts to achieve good pitch are a problem of personality and intelligence.

A-440—THE ORCHESTRAL PITCH STANDARD

There often exists a perennial disagreement between the oboist, who wishes to use the standard tuning A, based on 440 cycles per second, and the string player, who prefers his A a bit higher. The string players have a strong tendency to insist on the higher pitch, since the increased tension on the strings also produces a more brilliant, intense tone quality. The use, by the Boston Symphony Orchestra, of an A of 444 cycles per second and other professional orchestras tuning at 441, or 442 cycles per second, tends to make higher pitch a fad among conductors who are not capable of dealing with the resultant problems.

Most orchestras tune at either 440 cycles, or slightly higher—perhaps 441 or 442. The danger of a higher pitch than 442 lies in the tuning of the woodwind instruments. Most woodwinds are constructed with 440 cycles per second as a standard to which the entire tempered chromatic scale of the instrument is related. If a wind instrument is forced to tune much above or below that standard, the various registers will be forced apart or together. A higher pitch also forces the wind players to "pinch" and produce a smaller, constricted tone.

Perhaps the Boston Symphony wind players can travel to Paris or to their own repairman or manufacturer to have their instrument adjusted or constructed to their specifications so that they can use the higher pitch standard without impairing their performance. This is an unusual situation, however, and fortunately most orchestras are not trying to "upstage" the Boston Symphony with 445 c.p.s. or higher. For the conductor of a school or community orchestra, the wisest course is to stay as close to 440 as possible. John De Lancie, first oboist of the Philadelphia Orchestra expresses his resistance to a pitch above A-440 with the question, "Where does it end?"

Again, it is the conductor who must first decide on the best pitch for his orchestra, and then demand that the oboist, or an electronic tuning signal, produce that pitch, and that all members of the orchestra adhere to that pitch standard. The conductor who refuses to become involved while players battle over several concepts of the tuning note is inviting a very aggravating situation. And if he allows the orchestra to perform without resolving the conflict, thereby allowing more than one concept of pitch to exist simultaneously, he perhaps would be happier with players who are also not so concerned with the pitch problems. Such orchestras do exist, but they do not inspire a great deal of praise. Most serious orchestral musicians feel that unless the conductor constantly agitates for adherence to the pitch standard, even the finest orchestral players cannot solve the problems of tuning in the orchestra.

It should be understood that especially in a school orchestra, the students will look to the conductor for their leadership, and the leadership with regards to pitch can only come from the conductor of such an orchestra. Even the idea of a pitch standard might be foreign to the members of a student orchestra, and it is in such an orchestra where a fine concept of pitch can begin. It does not occur, however, unless the teacher/conductor is sensitive to pitch, and unless he continually keeps his students aware of the importance of listening and adjusting to each other.

USE OF AN ELECTRONIC A-440

The question of the source of the tuning note also arises. The tradition of using the oboist is questionable, since so many oboists, particularly among amateur players, do not produce a consistent A-440. Some conductors have taken a positive step towards solving the problem by using an electronic instrument to produce the tuning note. There are several such instruments available (see page 16) and they are far more reliable than most oboists. They also offer the additional advantage of taking the pressure off of the oboist. Most oboists welcome the relief. Leopold Stokowski, during his tenure as conductor of the Philadelphia Orchestra, used a mechanical tuning device with the orchestra at the Curtis Institute as early as 1938. The device had to be pumped, and had a tuning range from A-436 to A-442. Mr. Stokowsky used A-438.

Some conductors feel that it is not as "professional" to use such an artificial tuning note, and there are conductors who balk at using an electronically produced pitch even though their oboists might produce a different A at each rehearsal. Apparently, it is more important to such a conductor to "appear professional" by using an inconsistent oboist than it is to sound professional by having a consistent tuning note. It is my understanding that several of our major U. S. orchestras now use such an electronic A. It seems logical that each conductor must determine as best he can with what degree of consistency his oboist produces the tuning "A." If not to his satisfaction, then the conductor must insist on an electronically produced A. It is immensely important that the tuning note be consistent, not only from rehearsal to rehearsal, but from hour to hour in each rehearsal.

There are many orchestras—particularly community orchestras—in which the attention given to the tuning note is dreadfully lax. In such situations the oboist may give an accurate A, but many of the players use the A merely as sort of a perfunctory signal that the concert is about to begin. A renowned guest conductor remarked to the cello section of a community orchestra, "You might at least tune your open strings." This was not meant to be sarcasm. He had hit upon one of the great weaknesses of the orchestra. After the oboist had given the A, there was immediately a loud blast of A (A?) from all instruments, and the strings never had an opportunity to tune their open A string and the other open strings before that blast from the rest of the orchestra. Any orchestra, other than a fully professional one, will have a few string players who are not totally confident about tuning the open strings, and frequent checks by the conductor serve to impress on them the importance of striving for perfectly tuned open strings. Wind players are frequently even more careless. Not unusual is the situation in which the wind player arrives at the rehearsal too late for adequate warm-up, and his matching of the A is merely a momentary phase. Within a few minutes his pitch is much above 440, and in many situations the player makes no attempt to pull back to the standard.

PITCH AND TEMPERATURE

It must be remembered that the pitch of a wind instrument will rise more rapidly than the pitch of a stringed instrument because of the wind instrument's contact with the breath of the player. When the wind instrument is cold, it cools the air coming from the lungs, and sound travels slower in cold air, producing a lower pitch. The pitch rises with the temperature of the air inside the wind pipe.

As the instrument is warmed by both the room temperature and by the warmer temperature of the breath, the pitch rises higher than it does on a stringed instrument. The wind player must consequently be even more alert than the string player to changes in pitch resulting from a sustained playing situation and changes in temperature.

TEMPERED TUNING AND THE WIND INSTRUMENTS

An even more acute problem among some wind players is their failure to realize the importance of tempered tuning. Does a wind player use equal temperament (tempered tuning or the tempered scale) in playing in an orchestra or does he tune to pure intervals? The experienced wind player is aware that both systems of tuning are used in ensemble playing. The less sensitive wind player might answer that he tunes exclusively to pure intervals, (the term pure interval referring to ratios of 3/2, 4/3, 5/4, 6/5, etc., for the perfect 5th, perfect 4th, major 3rd, minor 3rd, etc., respectively), and that he has no need for equal temperament. As a system of tuning there is that somewhat unsavory aspect of equal temperament—its impurities—which makes such a player believe he should shun such a system. And he is correct insofar as he is applying this reasoning to a sustained harmonic situation involving traditional chords constructed in thirds. However, most wind passages in the orchestral literature rule out the possibility of tuning with pure intervals. (This applies to all levels of orchestral and band literature.) First, other than in very slow and sustained harmonic passages, the movement is too fast to allow most musicians to make any adjustment to pure harmony. Second, many melodic passages are also too fast to permit adjustment. Third, one of the greatest intonation challenges for the wind player is that of playing in unison or octaves with other wind players, which precludes the use of pure intervals in moving melodically from one note to the next, because, again, the passage is usually too fast, and there would be a need for both players to adjust with a common concept of the melodic interval. Finally, most current contemporary music, serial music in particular, rarely offers anything so "homey" for tuning as a major third. In such music, the player must rely on his concept of the note as it appears in his chromatic scale.

In each of the situations described above, wind players with a well-tuned tempered chromatic scale simply rely on that scale as their common ground. A remarkable event takes place when two extremely conscientious wind players from different parts of the country, both of whom have a finely tempered chromatic scale based on A-440 c.p.s. play together for the first time. Tuning problems are rare, and each player has an immediate respect for that aspect of his colleague's musicianship. Such a unified concept of intonation creates an unusually fine atmosphere for making music.

THE SOMEWHAT WELL-TEMPERED WIND INSTRUMENT

In addition it must also be noted that for good reason, instrument manufacturers, in striving for the most perfectly tuned wind instrument possible, always seek as their standard the tempered chromatic scale. For various acoustical reasons which a conductor should know, manufacturers never quite succeed (in spite of commercial claims), but they occasionally come close enough so that a sensitive wind player can learn to adjust such an instrument to a tempered scale. However, no two wind instruments—even two Heckel bassoons of the same series—will have the same discrepancies in their tempered scale. The wind player must get to know the discrepancies of his own instrument and the required adjustment necessary to achieve a well-tempered chromatic scale.

School band directors in particular must be aware of the importance of a wind instrument being tuned as closely as possible to the equally tempered scale. Most school musicians—certainly on the pre-college level, and perhaps even most musicians on the college level—do not develop a real sensitivity to pitch. Such pitch awareness would enable the student to adjust his instrument when necessary in correcting flaws in his instrument's tempered scale. A carelessly replaced pad on a saxophone can turn a half-step into a quarter tone, and this occurs more often than we would like to believe. Also, most valved brass instruments are played by students who do not understand the tuning slides, which should be used to get the best approximation of a tempered scale.

Beyond such problems as the difficulty of keeping the instrument in condition and properly adjusted, is the problem of trying to adjust to pure intervals, a problem which is discussed in more detail later in this chapter. In view of such problems within a school band we are faced with the additional harsh fact that most instruments owned by school musicians are not constructed according to the highest professional standards of pitch. And although the quality of wind instruments used in schools has improved considerably in recent years, there are still examples of "mail order house" purchases of instruments, "hand-me-downs" from a relative, instruments which are desperately in need of overhaul, even some companies which turn out questionable instruments, and the fact that the professionals get first choice of the best instruments made by the best companies.

Certainly with all of these pitfalls facing the conductor of a school band or orchestra, he should search for an instrument which has as few built-in tuning problems as possible.

If the conductor experiences unusual difficulties in tuning the winds of his orchestra—usually most evident in unison passages—he must find out which of his musicians have been exposed to the above, or similar ideas on equal temperament. Or in the case of a school orchestra, which of his students' instruments are relatively close to a tempered scale. If there is direct hostility to these ideas, then one must hope that the musicians with such an attitude are extremely gifted, and that they can play unison passages in tune without the aid of equal temperament. (It is my personal opinion that many of the players who reject equal temperament and claim to use only pure intervals, seem to use neither, and use "pure intervals" as an excuse to cover for their inability to tune to the other members of the ensemble. "Everyone is out of tune except me.")

If the conductor is not confronted with such an attitude, he can guide his musicians towards an improved tuning standard, using equal temperament as the guideline for tuning each player's instrument. On all levels of orchestral playing, wind instrument players will perform with a better concept of intonation if they know how near their instrument is to equal temperament.

Two additional points which are significant in regard to tempered tuning are: 1) It is generally accepted that the player tunes the instrument. If a musician is not careful, however, the instrument can "detune" the player. Continual exposure to a slightly out-of-tune note can make the player feel that the note is in tune. An occasional objective analysis of each note on the instrument to test its proximity to equal temperament—the goal which the manufacturer tried to achieve—is very revealing and helpful. 2) In spite of any imperfections which the tempered scale might have in tuning wind instruments, we must be aware that it is our best means of being nearest to acceptable intonation considering all of the keys and all of the musical situations encountered by wind players.

TUNING TO THE CHORD OF NATURE

The preceding dealt with the importance of tempered tuning in the orchestra. I wish to stress the fact that, although tempered tuning is of great importance, never should a conductor overlook the importance of tuning to pure intervals wherever possible.

At a recent state music educators' convention there was on display a model of the Johnson Intonation Trainer (see p. 20). This is one of a number of electronic tuning devices which have entered the market in recent years, and which will have a profound effect on concepts of intonation in the future. It is a small three octave keyboard, each tone of which is easily adjustable. The gentleman demonstrating asked many curious band directors to try their skill at tuning a perfect fifth. Towards the end of the day he lamented the fact that only two out of five of the directors were able to tune the fifth accurately.

A problem of not quite such serious proportions exists in many orchestras in which the conductor tolerates traditional sonorities (i.e., major triads, diminished 7th chords, etc.) played out of tune. A conductor should be aware of the acoustical ratio of the major triad, for instance, and the sound produced when that ratio is accurately produced. One can see and hear this vividly when the major triad is produced by electronic means (variable oscillators) with a connection to an oscilloscope. Until the 4 to 5 to 6 ratio of the root, third, and fifth is produced, the resultant sine wave on the oscilloscope is very disturbed. At the time when the triad is most sonorous, the sine wave becomes still.

The major chord, so tuned, is identical in frequency to the fourth, fifth and sixth partials of the harmonic series, with a ratio of four to five to six. Therefore, the major triad and other traditional chords built in thirds have a scientific basis for tuning, and tuning is less a subjective matter than most musicians think. Such chords cannot be left to chance, or to the vagaries of individual players of the orchestra. The conductor must have a keen ear for such sonorities, and he should not accept anything which is not pleasing to his own ear. Unfortunately, there is an alarming number of conductors—even in some of the most influential conducting positions in this country—who are not disturbed by an out-of-tune major chord.

The conductor will encounter this problem more with orchestral wind players than with string players. From the beginning of the string player's training he is taught to tune intervals without the aid of keys (buttons to push). He begins with unisons and perfect fifths (or 4ths) and must produce every interval with his ear as his only guide. Wind players with the exception of trombones are taught that a pitch is produced by pushing a certain button. Even trombonists are occasionally taught that 3rd position is about 3 and 3/4 inches beyond 2nd position. A perfect fifth between two young trumpet players means E—valves one and two—for one player, and B—valve 2—for the other, and not a certain pleasing sonority for which the ear is listening.

It is, however, possible for the string player to get used to putting the finger down in the same place for every situation, but there is also the initial challenge for him to learn to put his finger down in the first place through the guidance of his ear. As a result, most simple harmonic passages come through quite well in the strings (with the exception of very young string players) and seasoned string players generally play such harmonies with a good feeling for basic traditional sonorities.

Not so with wind players. Unless the player has had exceptional guidance, he has not been trained to adjust, for example, the third of a major chord, or the 7th of a major-minor 7th chord. Every conductor has had to work with wind players who have not learned to adjust intervals even after twenty years of experience.

ELECTRONIC TUNING AIDS

On the following pages are presented some of the electronic teaching aids which offer ideal opportunities for the conductor or the orchestral musician to test and improve his concept of pure intervals and of tempered tuning. This is by no means a complete list of such tuning aids, but merely some of the best known.

Several other electronic instruments have appeared on the market for a short time, only to be removed for reasons which are generally not known. Two such instruments, both of which contain excellent basic principles, are still to be found in the possession of various institutions and individuals. They are:

The Magna-tuner, which was distributed by H. & A. Selmer. A versatile instrument which produces one hundred and fifty-six different fixed tones and one hundred and forty-four intervals all selected by push-button; all twelve equally tempered tones over a three octave range; provision for sounding two tones simultaneously; fine tuning of the second tone to give equally tempered or just intervals; and adjustment of any of the tempered tones from A-438 to A-444 or equivalents.

The Tempo-tuner, also distributed by H. & A. Selmer. It consists of a metronome, set pitches of A, B flat, C and F, based on A-440, and another tone, or signal, which is variable. Only one tone can be sounded at one time, but in combination with another such device, or an instrument, this is very helpful.

The following instruments are currently available. The address of each manufacturer is also included.

The Peterson Chromatic Tuner, Model 70, manufactured by Peterson Electro-Musical Products of Worth, Illinois. The Chromatic Tuner, Model 70, is a very effective device. It contains all semitones of the chromatic scale tuned to the tempered scale, and should very well serve the purpose of aurally testing the accuracy of every note of an instrument to the tempered scale. It is transistorized and battery-operated.

THE PETERSON CHROMATIC TUNER MODEL 70

Courtesy Peterson Electro-Musical Products, Worth, Ill.

The Peterson Chromatic Tuner, Model 300, similar to the Peterson Model 70. This instrument has the additional advantages of seven octaves, as compared to the single octave of the model 70, and a vernier pitch control which is variable one half semitone sharp or flat from A-440. It is transistorized, operating on standard 105 to 125 volts A. C.

THE PETERSON CHROMATIC TUNER MODEL 300

Courtesy Peterson Electro-Musical Products, Worth, Ill.

The Peterson Strobe Tuner, Model 400, another handy and practical tuning device from the Peterson Company. It is a visual pitch calibrator, with a seven octave range, and an image clarifier for low notes which are usually difficult to see on such instruments. A single viewing window necessitates a dial adjustment for each pitch change in the chromatic scale. It is also transistorized, with a weight of only nine pounds, five ounces.

THE PETERSON STROBE TUNER MODEL 400

Courtesy Peterson Electro-Musical Products, Worth, Ill.

The Lectro-tuner, produced by Conn Corporation, and one of the most popular devices for producing an electronic A or B flat. Although it is almost always used strictly as a "canned tuning note," it has been proven very helpful for young instrumentalists in the development of their concept of pure intervals. Used in combination with an orchestral instrument, one can play and adjust intervals to develop pitch acuity. An awareness of a pleasing interval sound will develop when one discovers the difference between the intervals when played without care, and the same interval when played with the adjustment necessary to make it a pure interval. The idea of playing "duets" with such an electronic "A" may not appeal to some musicians, but it would help so many of them who are not sensitive to such a problem as a major third played slightly out of tune. Intervals should be produced both above and below the B flat and A.

THE LECTRO-TUNER

Courtesy Conn Corp., Elkhart, Indiana

The Stroboconn, an excellent pitch calibrator made by Conn. It has been in existence for many years, but its value is unfortunately overlooked by many musicians and music educators. It is a perfectly adequate means of testing the accuracy of the tempered scale of wind instruments. In the section of this chapter under *Tempered Tuning and the Wind Instruments,* the importance of tempered tuning was brought out. Since all wind instruments are constructed with certain intonation flaws, it is advisable that every wind player spend a great deal of time with such an instrument as the Stroboconn in order to find out which notes vary from equal temperament, and whether or not they can be mechanically corrected.

Brass players should be aware of which fingering is in tune or flat or sharp to equal temperament, and how best to adjust each valve tuning slide and the main tuning slide to produce the best tempered scale.

Woodwind players should also find out which fingerings are in tune and which are not. Woodwind players have the additional need of making an occasional check with such an instrument to find out if the wear on any cork has caused a pad to elevate and cause sharpness. It is surprising how much gradual wear will make a note sharp without the player being aware of it. Notes can also become flat if dust and grime are allowed to accumulate in a tone hole.

String players can also test their ability to match the tempered scale, although their freedom to control all notes except their open strings makes them less dependent on tempered pitch.

Occasionally one finds the Stroboconn in use in a school band or orchestra rehearsal. This seems to me to be not the ideal place for the instrument, as it restricts one to relating to tempered tuning. A wind player should know how this instrument relates to the tempered scale, but he should also be aware that the tempered scale is only a guide, and that he should listen for pure intervals as much as possible. The best use of the Stroboconn seems to be with one or two individuals in the practice room —testing the intonation of their own instruments.

THE STROBOCONN
Courtesy Conn Corp., Elkhart, Indiana

The Strobotuner, also by Conn; this is a simplified version of the Stroboconn. It is a bit unwieldly in comparison to the Stroboconn, however, since the operator must dial into view each pitch he wishes to calibrate. Whereas the Stroboconn has a viewer for each of the twelve notes of the chromatic scale, the Strobotuner has only one such viewer, and a dial adjusts it to the desired pitch. The instrument is highly desirable in the absence of a Stroboconn, however. The price is also considerably lower.

THE STROBOTUNER

Courtesy Conn Corp., Elkhart, Indiana

The Johnson Intonation Trainer, a versatile three octave keyboard instrument with adjustable pitches of about six semitones. There is also a beat indicator to indicate when a pure interval is perfectly tuned. A separate rank of tones tuned to the tempered scale is available by turning a switch. The use of such a device will certainly become universal in music schools within the next decade, since it can be used for aptitude tests, demonstrations of pythagorean, mean-tone and equal temperament tuning in theory or physics classes, and as a most effective ear training device. It is manufactured by E. F. Johnson Co., Waseca, Minnesota.

THE JOHNSON INTONATION TRAINER

Courtesy E. F. Johnson Company, Waseca, Minnesota 56093

Every conductor should take the time to work with the above mentioned instruments—particularly the Stroboconn, or Strobe Tuner, and the Johnson Intonation Trainer—to test his own concept of intonation under reliable conditions.

It is particularly important that no matter how much confidence a conductor or student conductor has in his innate ability to hear pitch, he should nevertheless experiment with these training aids. Frequently it is the person who thinks most highly of his ability to deal with intonation problems who learns most from the devices. A fine pianist, for example, who hears the progression of one chord to the next with great ease, might discover that he automatically accepted the intonation of the piano, not realizing the need to "control" the intonation of chords in the ensemble. A fine wind player who has developed great technical and expressive skill might discover that his ear has been conditioned to accept the false intonation of several notes on his instrument.

Some musicians with so-called "perfect pitch" or "pitch recognition"—the ability to sing or identify any note at any time—could also profit greatly from working with these instruments. Occasionally this ability leads a person to think that he might have a near-perfect sense of hearing. It is often such a person who has an unsure concept of the true intonation of octaves, unisons, and other intervals and triads.

And the musician who already has a position as conductor, no matter how long he has conducted, or on which level he conducts, might discover that his concepts of melodic and chordal sonorities—both natural and tempered—could be improved.

Chapter 3

Rhythmic Ensemble

LISTENING WHILE PLAYING

The term *rhythmic ensemble* refers to that split-second precision which is achieved only by extremely well-disciplined ensembles. It encompasses both of the elements which produce precision performances—absolute rhythmic accuracy and ensemble awareness on the part of each performer in the ensemble.

Let us first consider a formidable ensemble problem such as is found in the 5th movement (Presto) of Beethoven's quartet #14 in C♯ Minor—Op. 131. There is an almost continual sixteenth note pattern throughout the movement, with occasional relief found in the second theme which is of a more legato and less hectic nature. This is one of the most difficult movements in the string quartet literature in terms of ensemble because so much of the movement must relate to the rapid sixteenth notes. Voices enter and drop out while the sixteenths continue. Other themes are accompanied by sixteenths and must therefore relate to them. Solo voices carry sixteenths between themes. Proof of the difficulty is heard when a quartet of less than superior quality attempts the work. A work of such difficulty requires a truly brilliant ensemble group. In addition to the technical mastery—bringing forth every note with accuracy of pitch and articulation—each player must possess a rhythmic confidence and aggressiveness which will provide the impetus necessary for sustained excitement. On the other hand, any rhythmic flexibility—rubato, ritard, accelerando—is immediately sensed by all four players simultaneously. Again it is the double implication of our term rhythmic ensemble—rhythm *and* ensemble—which is important to the ensemble player and conductor, because it suggests rhythmic mastery and total awareness of the actions of the other ensemble members.

Great ensemble players, therefore, are not only fine virtuoso performers, they are virtuoso listeners as well. A conductor can accomplish gratifying results in converting non-listeners among his musicians into listeners if he approaches each rehearsal with this goal in mind. There is a direct relationship between the player's ability to hear and concentrate on other parts, and his proficiency as an ensemble musician.

THE CONDUCTOR'S RHYTHMIC MASTERY

We must, however, be able to assume that a high degree of rhythmic mastery exists on the part of the conductor. Without such mastery, the conductor is at the mercy of his orchestra, because there will be in almost any orchestra at least some musicians who are rhythmically secure—

21

and a display of insecurity or inaccuracy on the part of a conductor can undermine the musicians' confidence in him. This workbook will not deal with the problems of developing rhythmic mastery, as it is covered in any number of textbooks.

In chapter eight of this workbook will be found a number of examples of complex rhythmic patterns which can be used to test the conducting student's rhythmic skills, and to determine whether or not the student is sufficiently adept at rhythmic reading to prepare him for a study of conducting.

ENSEMBLE PLAYING AND RHYTHM

How can a conductor make his orchestra members more aware of good rhythmic ensemble? With orchestras in which all of the musicians are fully professional performers—earning their living primarily from orchestral playing—the rhythmic aspect of our problem should be virtually non-existent. Each player should have developed a high degree of rhythmic skill in his own way. The ensemble aspect of the problem, however, will exist with every orchestra, its solution depending on the ability of the conductor to put together the type of ensemble which he conceives.

With semi-professional and amateur orchestras, in which some players are rhythmically insecure, the problem of rhythm must be solved before the problem of ensemble can be intelligently approached. All non-professional orchestras have their share of players—most frequently found in second violin and viola sections—who do not play until they see what other people in their section will do. Hence, they play everything late. (My intention is not to criticize the fact that such players are permitted to play in orchestras, as I well recognize the need to encourage as many orchestral players as possible.) With such players it is nearly impossible to expect precise ensemble playing. Until they can be taught to play along with accurate rhythm—to be rhythmically aggressive and independent—there will be little chance of their concentrating any of their attention on another voice in the orchestra to produce precision ensemble.

Again, the solution to any player's rhythmic problems is a personal matter, and it is not the purpose of this workbook to suggest any new approaches to learning rhythm. On the other hand, the development of the musicians' ability to fit into an ensemble, as well as the development of the ability of a section to fit into the orchestra, is something which can and should be taught in each rehearsal. The conductor must use whatever method he can find to discover the rhythmic weaknesses of his musicians and to overcome such weaknesses. Only then will he be able to develop a sense of rhythmic ensemble in his orchestra.

The problem of instilling in an instrumental ensemble a strong sense of rhythm and rhythmic ensemble is three-fold. First, as we have already mentioned, the conductor must be rhythmically as adept as, or more adept than, any member of his orchestra. Second, he must be able to convey to his musicians through a very clear and precise baton technique the rhythmic concepts which are in his own mind. And third, he must instill in his musicians the habit of relating rhythmically to other voices within the orchestra—the listening habit.

The best ensemble musicians are those who, in performance, are most aware of voices other than their own. There are pianists who excel on the recital stage but who are not good accompanists because they are not trained to follow and adjust to another voice. An orchestral player must be able to adjust constantly in his role as accompanist to other members of the orchestra or to a soloist. The conductor who is fully aware of these facts will try to impart this sense of "ensemble awareness" to his musicians at every opportunity so that the practice of adjusting to other parts becomes habit with them.

IMPARTING ENSEMBLE AWARENESS

A few different steps for helping to convey such an ensemble awareness to orchestral musicians are suggested with the relatively simple example below.

EXAMPLE 1

An unconvincing interpretation of this passage may be due to a lack of understanding of its rhythmic construction, but a more likely reason is the inability of the players to relate their syncopated pattern to the pattern of notes falling on each beat. The following steps are suggested:

1. The syncopated figure should be omitted while the other voice is played alone. Those players who are omitting the syncopated figure should sing that pattern to themselves while listening to the other voice.

2. The syncopated figure should be played by one skilled player while the other voice is played. The other musicians who are omitting the syncopated part listen.

3. The players of the syncopated part then sing their part with the other part, using non-pitched syllables if necessary.

4. Both parts are sung, then played as written, and accompanied by a snare drum or other percussion instrument tapping audibly each eighth note of the measure. In this way each of the two groups have a definite beat and beat division to which to relate, and the evenness of the on-the-beat/off-the-beat sequence can be emphasized.

5. Any ensemble passage which presents a basic rhythmic problem for orchestral players should be rehearsed at a *greatly reduced tempo.* This enables the players to follow more accurately what is happening in another voice, while affording them more time to gain confidence on their own parts. If conductors and ensemble players could approach the learning of ensemble music as they would approach two-part melodic dictation in the theory class, improved ensemble performances would follow. Most musicians when faced with two-part melodic dictation would immediately ask for the parts to be played a number of times slowly *so that they could hear one part in relation to the other part.* Is this not the same problem facing the ensemble musician?

Although an extremely simple example has been used for our study here, there is no reason why the same technique could not be used in solving the rhythmic ensemble problems to be found in a difficult standard orchestral work. The following example from the finale of Mozart's *Symphony in C, "Jupiter"* K. 551, contains a number of varied rhythmic figures, a by-product of one of the finest examples of virtuoso fugal writing in the symphonic literature.

The example contains rather conventional rhythmic patterns, but so many varied rhythmic patterns are occurring simultaneously that—despite their individual simplicity—there is an inherent potential for unpolished and uncoordinated ensemble. If the conductor points out to the orchestra all of the various rhythmic figures which occur within the four measures and then points out the

EXAMPLE 2 from Mozart's *Symphony in C, "Jupiter"* K. 551

relationship between each rhythmic figure and the most elementary rhythmic pattern relating to the sub-divided beat (in this case the pattern of eighth notes) a much better understanding of the rhythmic ensemble problems of the movement can be achieved.

EXAMPLE 3

MOZART: SYMPHONY IN C — JUPITER
FINALE — ALLEGRO MOLTO

(The use of string parts only is due to the fact that the wind instruments are for the most part duplicating the strings at this point, or playing more sustained passages of half and whole notes.)

The following example (page 26) shows the relationship of each note of the various rhythmic passages to the basic rhythm of alla breve time—eight eighth notes. A conductor can make his musicians more aware of this relationship of rhythms not through the visual process shown, but by: 1) explaining the different rhythms so that his musicians will know what to listen for; 2) demonstrating through the use of various voice combinations (e.g., second violin and cello, or bass and viola, etc.) the rhythmic relationships involved; and 3) slowing the passage to a tempo which will enable each player to carefully listen and become familiar with the other voices.

Using the same approach as was used in example 1, we shall consider the varied problems which occur in an entire composition. The *Variations on a Theme of Haydn*, Op. 56a, by Brahms has been selected, since it offers a variety of rhythmic relationships in the several variations. *The reader should have a score of the work in hand before reading this section.*

EXAMPLE 4   Rhythmic Analysis of Example 3

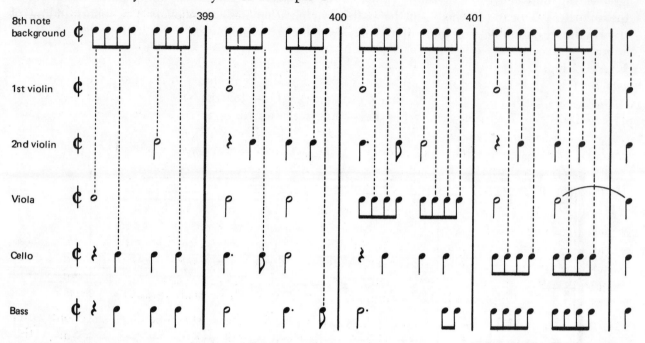

Brahms: Variations on a Theme of Haydn

Theme: The theme is very straightforward and offers no complex ensemble problem. A very common problem, however, the value of the dotted eighth and sixteenth figure, might occur. It should present little problem for any orchestra if the players are made aware of the relationship of the figure ♪♪ to the more fundamental figure ♫♫.

Var. I: There are three rhythmic patterns which must be synchronized in a clean performance of the first variation.

EXAMPLE 5

The passage should be broken down so that in the first four measures the eighth notes can be heard against the quarter notes without the distraction of the triplets. If the triplet passage is omitted, the musicians with the eighth note pattern will begin to depend on the quarter note pattern and listen for it. Once accomplished, the eighth note pattern can be omitted while the triplet pattern is played, giving those musicians who have the triplet pattern an opportunity to hear and to concentrate on the quarter-note pattern. In the second four measures the instrumentation is somewhat reversed from that of the first four measures. The dissecting should once more occur to give the players the opposite experience, i.e., playing triplets against the quarters instead of eighths against quarters. Since the remainder of the first variation is filled with duplet-triplet figures, the same approach can be used as needed throughout the variation. Conceivably in at least one rehearsal, the timpanist could be asked to continue his quarter note passage throughout the entire variation for purposes of emphasizing the quarter pattern.

The reason behind this approach is that once a musician is aware of the most uncomplicated pattern to which he can relate his part, he then has a greater chance of fitting perfectly into an ensemble. After all, is this not what a conductor does in giving a beat to which all voices can relate? He certainly could not conduct the triplets, eighths and quarters at one time. In the above case, the quarter note pattern becomes the "aural conductor." Each player is relating to the quarter note as a common focal point, although a common focal point which he hears rather than sees.

Var. II: Whereas in variation I, the quarter note served as the most simple and fundamental unit to which all other rhythmic patterns related, in the second variation the eighth note assumes this role. With the exception of a few measures, the eighth note pattern continues throughout the variation. The presence of the eighth note pattern can be immediately emphasized in a rehearsal by having the cellos and basses play the first repeated section alone. If necessary the rest of the variation can be performed with instruments entering only when they have the eighth note pattern. Several improvements in the ensemble interpretation will result from this emphasis on the eighth note pattern. First, the dotted eighth-sixteenth figure will more likely be interpreted correctly, rather than as a triplet. Second, the numerous releases of the eighth note which follow the quarter will be more precise, since the musicians will feel two eighths while holding the quarter and then moving to the following eighth note. Third, the dove-tailing in the strings at the beginning of the second repeated section will be more exact and more smooth. This passage should be thoroughly rehearsed with the dove-tailing instruments playing alone.

Var. III: The sixteenth notes alternating between first and second flutes, first and second bassoons, violas, and cellos, etc., present the only serious problem in this variation. The simple and fundamental rhythmic unit which serves as a guide for all rhythm of the variations should also be the eighth note, and if those musicians who later play the sixteenth will concentrate very carefully on the eighth note during the opening measures of the variation, the sixteenth will remain more consistent. The nature of the sixteenth note passages are such, however, that they lend themselves to very pliable rhythmic interpretation, and frequently the passages are played too mechanically. The conductor must encourage his musicians to play the passage as flexibly and expressively as possible without dragging the rhythm.

Var. IV: Since there is an almost constant use of both eighth notes and sixteenth notes throughout this variation, the relationship between the two rhythms can immediately be clearly established. The problem throughout this variation is not one of knowing which rhythm one should relate to, but one of actually relating to (concentrating on) the contrasting rhythmic figure.

Var. V: This variation has the same type of complexity which was mentioned in relation to the 5th Movement (Presto) of Beethoven's Quartet #14 in C# minor—Op. 131. (See page 21.) It is technically difficult and requires superb bowing and articulation technique on the part of all musicians. It is made rhythmically complex through the unusual use of groups of two eighth notes in 6/8 pattern, where groups of three are usually expected.

The major problem is to keep the feeling of a continuous eighth note pattern moving throughout the variation. Since all of the orchestral voices have varied patterns based on the continuous eighth note movement, but no voice continues consistent eighth note movement for more than a measure or two without a rest, a *sforzato,* or an unusual melodic grouping of the notes, it is difficult to find a common eighth note to which all of the musicians can relate. In this case the conductor must be brash enough to add a snare drum to the variation for a rehearsal or two. The snare drum can play the eighth note pattern throughout the variation until each player has a greater feeling for the position of each of his notes in relation to the other voices. It might be compared to putting chalk marks on the floor for an actor until he developed security in a certain blocking. It is interesting to hear how many of the professional recordings of this variation do not display any great degree of precision. This is also an ideal example of a fast movement which must first be learned at a slow tempo. It is a similar ensemble problem to that which was found in the Mozart *"Jupiter" Symphony.* (See p. 24, Ex. 2.)

Var. VI: The most exhilarating performances of this variation give the impression of an incessant sixteenth note pattern which is simply turned on and allowed to run until stopped abruptly by the final sforzato. Anything that can imbue the musicians with a stronger feeling for the consistency and resultant power of the sixteenth in this variation will improve the performance. Again, as in variation V, the conductor might find it helpful to add a snare drum for one rehearsal. The snare drum would play straight sixteenth notes throughout the movement, observing only dynamic contrasts. This would exaggerate the aggressive quality of the movement and assist all of the musicians in their feeling for the placement of each sixteenth of the movement.

Var. VII: If the dotted eighth-sixteenth-eighth ♪♫ ♪ pattern in this variation can be uniformly interpreted by each player, and if the same pattern can be played with precision against the quarter-eighth or the running eighth note pattern, ensemble problems should not be too severe. Frequently the pattern is interpreted as ♪♫ ♪, adding more rhythmic vitality. Again, the practice of dissecting is helpful. First, using the beginning five measures only, the flute, viola, cello and bass parts are played without the rest of the orchestra. Then the remaining instruments play their part while flute, viola, cello and bass rest during the first five measures. If the musicians are encouraged to listen and to imagine their parts while resting, they will not only develop a better feeling for the rhythmic ensemble, but they will also develop a sense of the relative importance of their own parts.

Var. VIII: The problems in this variation are somewhat similar to those in Var. V. The tempo is fast, and a continuously moving eighth note is necessary for the spirit of the variation. The problems are compounded by a thinner texture and lighter dynamic level. The solution must result from the same approaches taken in the previous variations—isolating of parts, the addition of an instrument such as the snare drum to make the musicians more aware of consistent eighth notes, and starting with a greatly reduced tempo and increasing the tempo gradually.

Finale: The beginning of the finale, like the opening theme, is of a very basic rhythmic construction. It begins as a chaconne, continuing as such until the theme recurs in measure 465. The repeated ground bass creates a solid pattern to which other voices can relate, and for this reason it seems quite logical that any rehearsal of the finale should begin with the presentation of the ostinato figure by itself, allowing all musicians to become familiar with it.

The first rhythmic problem occurs with the entrance of the quarter note triplets. This can be solved easily if the conductor emphasizes beats one and three almost to the exclusion of beats two and four. Some measures later, at measure 385, the texture becomes thicker through the use of more eighth notes, which must be pointed out as the most predominant rhythmic "guide." At 391 six-teenth notes appear and later at 396 triplet sixteenths, both of which will relate to the eighth note patterns. At 401, quarter, eighths and triplets appear as in variation one. The very moderate tempo and consistency of rhythms in the finale do not present quite the complexity of problems as are found in the variations.

MORE COMPLEX RHYTHMIC ENSEMBLE PROBLEMS

Let us now consider rhythmic ensemble problems of a more complex nature. In much 20th cen-tury music we find irregular meter signatures used alternately with more common patterns, e.g., 2/4 —5/8—2/4, etc. Such rhythms occasionally create problems which are insurmountable to a great num-ber of orchestras, due to the lack of exposure on the part of many musicians—including conductors —to these unusual rhythms. In such cases it is quite helpful to create an original exercise which isolates the rhythmic problem from other problems within the passage such as virtuoso technical de-mands, difficult articulation and phrasing, etc., which might preclude the musician focusing his entire attention on the rhythmic problem.

A meter such as 5/8 time, which is today no longer the unwelcome stranger which it was two decades ago, can be approached in a manner which takes the rhythmic problem out of con-text and makes it more comprehensible to the musicians. Assuming that the musicians are having difficulties with the rhythm, the conductor, rather than plunging directly into the problem as it appears in the work, should take the musicians slowly through it just to get an initial exposure to the difficult passage. He should then begin his original exercise with repeated measures of 5/8 time, using a simple melodic pattern such as

EXAMPLE 6

Even the above pattern could be simplified for the musicians by having them count, read with syl-lables, or tap the pattern with one hand. The pattern should first be approached slowly, with each eighth note receiving one beat, then the tempo should increase gradually until two unequal beats are used in each measure, as in the following examples 7 and 8,

EXAMPLE 7   **EXAMPLE 8**

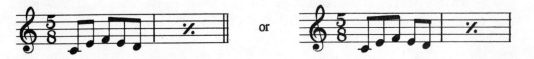

with two unequal beats per measure utilized.

The conductor might then add further examples, such as those which follow, gradually in-creasing the complexity of the musical problems within 5/8 meter.

EXAMPLE 9

EXAMPLE 10

Further steps might include the addition of simple contrapuntal parts, necessitating the development of ensemble awareness in relatively simple examples.

EXAMPLE 11

It is the gradual exposure to the new problem which will make the individual orchestral player more responsive to the meter, and more secure.

Each conductor should remember that in exploring a meter such as five-eight time, the composer will rarely present that meter in its most simple form. It is the conductor's responsibility to approach such a rhythm so that the musicians do not find it overwhelming. No lesser service can be done to a fine contemporary work than to play it unconvincingly. This is frequently a matter of the musicians' attitude. One occasionally meets a superbly trained musician whose playing of pre-20th century is of the highest calibre, but who has difficulties with such a meter as five-eight —often due to an aversion to modern music. Another of the conductor's responsibilities is to select the best music which uses such rhythmic complexities, and to see that the music is played in such a convincing manner that the musicians will enjoy it, and develop a taste for such music.

Chapter 4

Orchestral Balance

Developing a concept of orchestral balance, like developing a concept of orchestral tone, is a problem of perceptive exposure. There are very few teaching aids on balance such as there are on tuning which can be offered to the student conductor. If the student listens to and performs in enough orchestras, and if he takes full advantage of his experiences, he should develop a reasonably good perspective on this problem.

DYNAMIC POTENTIAL OF EACH INSTRUMENT

The experiences of orchestral musicians indicate that the primary weakness of conductors regarding balance is their frequent inability to recognize the dynamic potential of individual instruments and sections in the orchestra. String players are frustrated by the conductor's failure to demand a soft accompaniment in the winds. Woodwind players are likewise frustrated when they have the solo passage. It seems that only the brass and percussion have the power to simply sound above any accompanying passage.

How unfortunate such an imbalance is, since the orchestra is deprived of the real expressive value to be gained from dynamic contrasts! The extended clarinet solo in Rachmanninoff's *Second Symphony* has a dynamic range from pianissimo to forte. Frequently the clarinetist cannot use even a piano dynamic level because the conductor does not demand a soft string accompaniment. As a result, the dynamic nuances cannot be brought out, or else the solo is lost when the performer tries to play "*p*" as indicated in the score.

Conductors who refuse to make musicians play according to the pianissimo potential of their instrument when called for are inviting a loss of expressive quality in their orchestra. No individual stringed instrument has the power to play over a large number of brass, or woodwinds or other strings. The conductor should not always ask the soloist to "bring out the solo" as is too frequently done, because, more often than not, the answer lies in subduing the accompanying figure. This is a great discouragement to the finest players in an orchestra—and most damaging to the esteem of the conductor.

ENSEMBLE AWARENESS

The problem of balance is closely related to the problem of ensemble awareness discussed in the preceding chapter. If all orchestral players were aware of ensemble to the point of concentrating on other voices, and of being aware of the relative importance of their own voice, they would not treat a passage of accompanying quarter notes as though it were a prominent passage. The admonition, "if you do not hear the solo you are too loud," is excellent, but it must be supported by the conductor's insistence that each player, when accompanying, learn to give way dynamically for the solo voice.

The finest orchestral players, because of their vast experience, do many things instinctively that must be instilled into less experienced players. This statement is especially true in regards to orchestral balance. If one could select the finest one hundred players in the country for his own special orchestra, the most obvious balance problems would never appear, because the musicians would have learned through experience where to project, and where not to project. However, even with this select group the conductor would have to instill a new sense of dynamic consciousness in dealing with subtleties of balance, based on his own concept of each score he conducts and the overall sound he desires.

INHERENT BALANCE PROBLEMS OF EACH INSTRUMENT

Conductors should become familiar enough with each instrument of the orchestra that they know in which range the instrument will project and in which range it cannot easily project.

The flute's lowest range, particularly the bottom three or four notes, can be obscured by almost any orchestral sound. Its high A, on the other hand, will penetrate most orchestral sounds. The oboe quite naturally produces a penetrating tone. And it is necessary only to observe an orchestra in warm-up, to realize how the piccolo can project above the sound of all other orchestral instruments. The bassoon does not possess this natural tendency to project; it is therefore crucial that the conductor give special attention to accompaniments so that they do not cover the bassoon solos. With the viola section, due to the range of viola parts, the quality of strings in that range which do not project, and the weakness of the viola players in most orchestras, special attention must be given to important viola lines to assure that they are adequately heard.

Brass instruments under usual circumstances rarely have difficulties being heard; but when played with mutes, they must be treated more like the other solo instruments. A muted trumpet passage marked "piano" must be played with the force of a forte passage in order to project. Generally, the brass instruments are not as penetrating in their lower registers, and the problem of brass staccato is particularly acute in the low register.

KNOWLEDGE OF ORCHESTRATION

These are just a few of the major considerations involved in orchestral balance. They are orchestration problems, and this fact points out one of the most important areas of training for a conductor—that of composition and orchestration. All of the points brought out in this discussion on instruments are thoroughly covered in a basic orchestration class. Some of the finest conductors are those who have also composed and who have experienced the problems of orchestral balance, as well as other instrumental problems.

BALANCING THE ENTIRE ORCHESTRA

Thus far the problem of orchestral balance has been confined to a discussion of individual instruments and sections. The more sensitive problem of balancing the overall sound of an orchestra, although related directly to the relative strength of individual instruments, is more a problem of development of the conductor's own concept of orchestral sound. It is one of those illusive goals which is quite likely more dependent on the conductor's basic talent and desire than anything else.

Earlier in this workbook (page 5) reference was made to two recordings of Brahms' Third Symphony in F Minor, Op. 90. One is by Serge Koussevitzky and the Boston Symphony (RCA Victor LM 1025) and the other is by Leopold Stokowski and the Houston Symphony (Murry Hill SDBR 3030). This comparison offers a striking contrast between the way in which two conductors approach the relative importance of melodic line and accompanying line. As compared to the relative equality of melody and accompaniment in the Koussevitzky recording, the accompanying lines in the Stokowski version are almost inaudible.

Chapter 5

Articulation- The Winds

The problem of articulation, from the conductor's point of view, is one of knowing the capabilities of all of the wind instruments, and of establishing common concepts towards which all of his wind players strive. As with string bowing, one can learn a great deal about the articulation problems of each member of the brass and woodwind families by referring to numerous method books on each instrument, by discussing the problems with skilled performers on these instruments, and best of all, by learning to play some of the wind instruments.

The problem of imparting a like concept to all wind players in an orchestra is a much greater problem than it is with strings, due to the diverse acoustical nature of so many instruments. Not only will the trumpet player have a different technique than the oboist for approaching a certain passage, but the clarinetist may approach a passage in a manner which does not agree with that of the bass clarinetist. And there are different schools of thought on the same instruments: I have heard French horn players say never to start a note with the breath (without the tongue), and others say that such a method for starting a note is commonly used.

We will not explore methods of articulating each of the wind instruments, since this information is well documented elsewhere. Our purpose is rather to present throughout this workbook ideas on general fundamental orchestral problems as they present themselves to the conductor—in this case, articulation.

With members of a fully professional orchestra, most of the basic problems have long since been solved through previous orchestral experiences. Other orchestras will contain brass and woodwind players who have missed some of the elementary foundational techniques of wind articulation, and it is in this situation where the conductor will have to rely on his own knowledge of wind instrument articulation. The reader might wonder at this point, that if the second trumpet player, for example, after playing the trumpet for a number of years, did not learn how to produce a short staccato, how can the conductor, who is perhaps a violinist, learn such details in addition to all of the other details which he, as conductor, must learn? The answer to this question is that if the trumpet player did not learn to make a short staccato in that length of time, the young conductor has to be twice as resourceful as the trumpeter, more perceptive as a listener, and infinitely more desirous of knowing how an orchestra is made to sound good. If not, then both he and the trumpeter should question their orchestral involvement. If the conductor has sufficient talent and drive, he can quite thoroughly understand such a problem as trumpet articulation. If not, his chances of success are not bright.

STARTING AND STOPPING THE NOTE (ATTACK AND RELEASE)

A practical opening question on the subject of wind articulation is: How should the following passage be tongued? $\frac{2}{4}$ ♫ ♫ It could be tongued in three different ways, depending on tempo and the instruments involved. At an adagio tempo certain instruments start each eighth note by removing the tongue from the reed or teeth (a "tah" syllable). Other instruments use a breath attack ("hah") for starting each note. The ending of each note at this tempo is produced by discontinuing the force of air. At a somewhat faster tempo—moderato or allegretto—each player starts the note by removing the tongue from the reed or teeth, and ends the note by stopping the column of air. At a very rapid tempo the tongue serves to start and stop the note almost simultaneously. The latter is a concept which is rejected by some wind players, who claim that the notes should never be stopped with the tongue. It is true that the idea of avoiding the tongue completely in stopping a note is excellent, for it is too easy to produce a raucous effect in using the tongued release, especially with younger musicians, and this must be the principal consideration in this matter. On the other hand, rapid staccato passages most often make too much of a demand on the breathing apparatus to affect a breath or throat release. (Finally, there would seem to be no right or wrong method, since our major orchestras are filled with players of both schools of thought.) The conductor should above all be aware of the sound of good articulation, so that he can demand the highest standards of his players. If one wind player is not producing clean articulation, the conductor must detect this problem and undertake the necessary steps to correct it.

COMBINATIONS OF SLURRED AND STACCATO NOTES

The problem of stopping the notes with the tongue or breath appears again in connection with the ending of the final note of a slurred group such as the following group of slurred sixteenths:

EXAMPLE 12

This figure is automatically interpreted by some wind players as:

EXAMPLE 13

and by others as

EXAMPLE 14

However, the interpretation of the passage must depend on the conductor's concept of the passage, which in turn is influenced by his knowledge of what the wind instruments are capable of doing both individually and collectively.

A general rule followed by wind players in the interpretation of short groups of slurred notes, such as those of the preceding example, is that if the last of the slurred notes is followed by a staccato note, the last slurred note is clipped short with the tongue so as to leave as much space or silence as possible, in order to emphasize the approaching staccato note. The figure:

EXAMPLE 15

is consequently interpreted as

EXAMPLE 16

This interpretation applies primarily to livelier tempi, since it produces an unmusical effect when used at a slower tempo. Again the use of the tongue as a means of stopping the note is not accepted by some wind players. The important point remains, however, that the note preceding the staccato is shortened in the most clean and musical manner.

If the final slurred note is followed by a legato note or another slurred group such as:

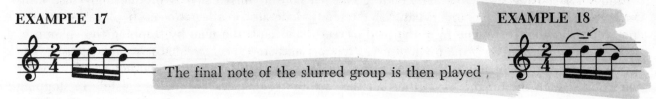

EXAMPLE 17

EXAMPLE 18

The final note of the slurred group is then played

with only a slight interruption of the sound with the tongue.

RAPID STACCATO

A conductor should also know the limits of articulation speed of each wind player in his orchestra, as well as what the wind instrument itself can be expected to do.

Brass players and flautists, for instance, are generally capable of double tonguing (producing two notes with one complete movement of the tongue). This enables them to execute rapid staccato—especially repeated notes—at a brilliant tempo. The double reeds are capable of double tonguing only in the hands of (mouths of) highly skilled players. I have met only a few single reed players who could use a double tonguing technique, and most of them could use it effectively only in certain registers of their instruments.

At what tempo, for example, can an orchestra perform the finale of Mendelssohn's *Italian Symphony*, or Rossini's *Thieving Magpie* Overture? Many orchestras would have to play either work at such a slow tempo in order to accommodate the slow staccato of some of their wind players that it might be more musical to select another composition. Many conductors program such works in spite of the inability of their wind players to reach their expected tempo. Results:

1. The conductor becomes very angry when he discovers his wind players cannot articulate the passage at his tempo, and he blames the winds instead of his own lack of foresight.
2. The conductor must go through with the programming as planned because he discovers the problem too late. The tempo is then taken either too slowly to be exciting or too rapidly to be executed with clarity.

All of this can be avoided if the conductor makes it a point to know the articulation capabilities of his players. Which ones can double tongue? Which ones can double tongue in a clean and crisp manner throughout the range of their instruments? Of those who are limited to a single tonguing technique, which ones are severely limited in the speed of their rapid staccato? At which tempo (m.m.) can the wind section collectively produce a clean interpretation of a scale passage such as the following:

EXAMPLE 19

This tempo becomes the approximate upper limit for any rapid staccato sixteenth note passage. It will range from about m.m. 112 or more with the good high school orchestra to about 126-132 in a semi-professional orchestra and about 152 or more in a professional orchestra. At which tempo can the same passage be played by individual members of the wind section? In which range does each player's articulation become unclear? If a wind player cannot produce a clean, short staccato, does the conductor recognize this fact, and prescribe remedial exercises or instructions? It is the conductor whose concept of orchestral articulation is hazy, who permits sloppy craftsmanship. A conductor who has a mental picture of George Szell's Cleveland Orchestra winds doing the scherzo of Mendelssohn's *Midsummernight's Dream* has such a lofty goal that this very goal might be forever unattainable by him. On the other hand, it will insure that he will never become complacent about his orchestral winds.

Chapter 6

Bowing–The Strings

Although string bowing and wind instrument articulation are related as to their controlling the length and grouping of notes, conductors must be aware of the much greater influence which bowing has on the orchestra, since the bow is also the tone-producing means on a stringed instrument. Most conductors who have played a stringed instrument, or who have otherwise immersed themselves in the problems of string playing, are aware of this and will make tone a major consideration when a problem of bowing appears.

If the conductor is a non-string player who conducts a community or semi-professional orchestra, he will most likely have a concert master who is capable of determining the best bowing. Most college orchestras will be able to rely on the guidance of a member of the string faculty of that institution. In fact, it is ironic that in the area where the influence of an experienced string player is most needed—the public school orchestra—there is frequently no one with the necessary background in stringed instruments. It is in such a situation that the conductor must seek the help of private teachers, bringing in local string teachers whenever possible, and definitely encouraging all of his string players to study privately with such a person.

Such problems as string crossing vs. changing position, which part of the bow to use to best achieve a desired effect, the type of stroke to use in a given technical passage, (i.e., on the string vs. spiccato, etc.), are problems which require the guidance of a string player, or one who has an otherwise extensive background with such problems. Again, however, we must conclude that much is dependent on the conductor's concept of how a string section should sound, and his willingness and desire to initiate whatever steps are necessary to achieve that which satisfies his expectations.

THE SOUND OF STRINGS

Almost every musician has experienced a concert of a school or amateur orchestra in which many of the string players use no more than one third of the bow throughout the concert, producing a most unsatisfying sound. It is true that much of this can be plainly attributed to the lack of experience or lack of talent on the part of such players. On the other hand, it is not uncommon that this is due to a lack of awareness on the part of the conductor. The same trait which permits a conductor to tolerate an oboist with a hard, raspy sounding reed, and a snare drummer whose drum-head sounds water-logged, will allow such bowing timidity among string players. Frequently the same timid players who shy away from a difficult allegro sixteenth note passage approach the final fortissimo whole note with the same hesitancy. It has been my observation that in an amateur orchestra there is a rather close parallel between the aggressiveness with which the string players bow, and the enthusiasm with which the conductor approaches his task.

KNOWING THE CAPABILITIES OF EACH PLAYER

One weakness which occurs in the non-professional orchestra—more frequently in the case of the community orchestra than with the school orchestra—is the conductor's lack of knowledge of the bowing capabilities of the individual string players. This is a problem which should have most significant bearing on the selection of music for programming. Should the conductor be unfamiliar with, for example, the spiccato capabilities of the members of his violin section, he would be unwise to consider most of the Haydn symphonies until he looks into the matter.

The entire matter of seating—which is important to an orchestra far beyond the pride of the individual players involved—should not be decided until the conductor knows the bowing capabilities of the individual players. The same problem which was described in relation to wind articulation in the preceding chapter—the selection of literature which is beyond the technical ability of the musicians—applies to string players. The conductor will avoid a great deal of aggravation if he knows what his string players are capable of performing before he selects literature for his musicians.

The conductor should also be alert to any weaknesses among his string players which might be corrected with remedial exercises or a private teacher. Such problems as tenseness, an improper bow grip, careless positioning of the bow on the strings, etc., if detected by the conductor might be corrected, especially in younger players. Certainly such alertness is mandatory in a school orchestra, where the conductor frequently has the sole responsibility for the musical development of the string player.

EDITING THE MUSIC

The conductor should be aware of the importance of editing music, not only to achieve what he considers to be a more authentic interpretation of the work, but to make a given passage better suited to the abilities of his own orchestra. Changes in a particular edition might be considered for the following reasons:

1. The music might have been poorly edited by the publishers.
2. The editor (or composer) might have conceived his particular edition for an advanced professional orchestra. In regards to long phrases which can be performed with a full sound only by a fine professional orchestra, it is frequently necessary to break up the phrases for a less proficient orchestra. This is especially true with the music of composers of the Romantic Period.
3. A conductor might have a special weakness within his orchestra which must continually be obscured by clever editing. For example, in the case of a weak viola section, short, difficult passages might be improved by adding one cello or one stand of violins, if the range permits. In the case of a weak viola line in a tutti orchestral passage, an additional clarinet can support a viola line without damaging the overall sonority. It is also frequently helpful to break a passage into two divisi passages to simplify it. In the case of a passage which calls for a change of position or string crossing for just one or two isolated notes, one or two stands or another section can play such notes, if they do not break up a phrase which could only be musically expressed by the intended section. The following example illustrates this technique.

EXAMPLE 20

Instead of playing the part as originally written, the violas play the substitute g and a, and the violins play the original g and a.

Such changes, though perhaps disturbing to the musical purist who would have nothing changed from the original edition, are necessary to enable a non-professional orchestra to give its best interpretation of a work.

4. The conductor might have a different concept of the passage, necessitating a different approach to a problem such as bowing. In the second example below, the crescendo on beats three and four might be much more convincingly executed through the additional bow stroke.

EXAMPLE 21   **EXAMPLE 22**

Note {

Another example of editing which might be based solely on the conductor's preference is the use of several contrasting bowing patterns within one section to achieve the effect of continuous bowing.

It would be beyond the scope of this workbook to compile a list of bowing problems and their solutions here. There is a great deal of instructional material available on bowing problems, particularly in basic violin and cello method books. Some suggestions for prospective conductors, especially those whose experiences with the stringed instruments are limited, which would broaden their concepts regarding the string instruments are:

1. Study a stringed instrument, though recognizing that your initial attempts will seem very unmusical.

2. Prepare your own bowings of violin solo works and orchestral excerpts and take them to a qualified string player for evaluation. Discuss why you suggest a certain bowing, and if he does not agree, ask why he suggests another.

3. Work with younger string orchestras (elementary) when the opportunity arises. You may develop confidence by learning with youngsters.

4. Attend concerts, recitals (especially of string chamber music), seminars, private lessons, etc., whenever possible.

5. When you conduct an orchestra, work with the concertmaster if he is a competent violinist so as to understand bowing problems in the works which are programmed.

6. Consult string instructional books on bowing and bowing problems. Two such works, *Orchestral Bowing and Routines*, by Elisabeth A. H. Green, and *Principles of Violin Playing and Teaching*, by Ivan Galamian, are listed in the bibliography.

PART II

BATON TECHNIQUE AND ITS APPLICATION

INTRODUCTION

Before becoming involved with the conducting exercises, it should once more be stressed that the purpose of this workbook is not only to develop a secure baton technique, but also to make the student conductor aware of and sensitive to musical problems which face conductors in every rehearsal. We are more interested in what happens to the student's ear than in what happens with his baton during the time he is involved with these materials.

It is, therefore, imperative that the teacher of any such course which makes use of this workbook be aware of and sensitive to musical problems. If not, he might permit the student conductor to apply a satisfactory baton technique with musicians who are producing unsatisfactory musical results. The student must demand precise attacks, well balanced chords, finely tuned triads, the best possible tone quality, smooth crescendos, precision ensemble, tasteful interpretation, etc., and in most cases, the teacher will have to continually apply pressure to the student until he develops more of this type of awareness and musical responsibility.

Without this attention to musical details, we are faced with the risk of training mere time-beaters rather than conductors.

Chapter 7

Organization of the Ensemble

SEATING

The following seating arrangement is recommended for each ensemble of three performers and conductor. It is designed to approximate the seating arrangement of an orchestra, in which the main melodic body, the violins, is at the conductor's left, the woodwinds and violas are in front of him, and the bass instruments are to his right.

SEATING ARRANGEMENT

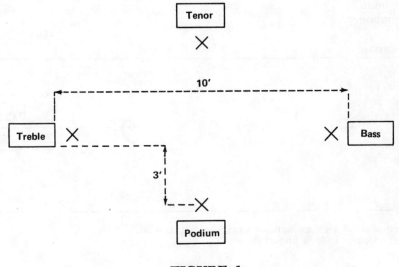

FIGURE 1

It is important that the treble and bass instruments are not seated too near each other, since the conductor would then not experience the problem of conducting to his left and to his right. This is an important part of working with an ensemble. A student might find it simple to cue on beats one and three, where there are no directional problems, but he might find it quite another problem to cue basses to the right on beat one, and violins to the left on beat three.

I also strongly recommend that a podium always be made available for the class. What are the psychological implications of stepping *up* onto a podium for the first time? One also steps *up* to appear on a witness stand, to deliver a sermon, to play the first solo, to enter the boxing ring, and even to face the gallows. With all of the problems confronting a young conductor in his first conducting experience, it might be of great help to eliminate as far as possible any aversion, conscious or subconscious, which he might have about mounting the podium for the first time.

INSTRUMENTATION

The following table indicates the instruments and range to be used with each voice of the ensemble.

TABLE 1

Treble
  flute
  clarinet (B flat)
  oboe
  violin
  viola
  soprano saxophone
  alto saxophone
  trumpet (C or B flat)

Tenor
  clarinet (B flat)
  alto clarinet (E flat)
  English horn
  violin
  viola
  cello
  alto saxophone
  tenor saxophone
  bassoon
  French horn

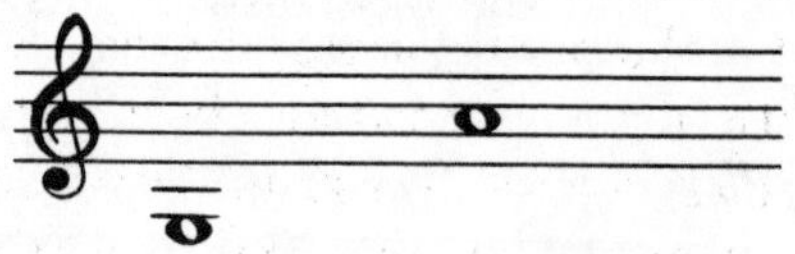

Bass
  bass clarinet
  bassoon
  baritone saxophone
  cello
  baritone horn
  trombone
  tuba*
  string bass**

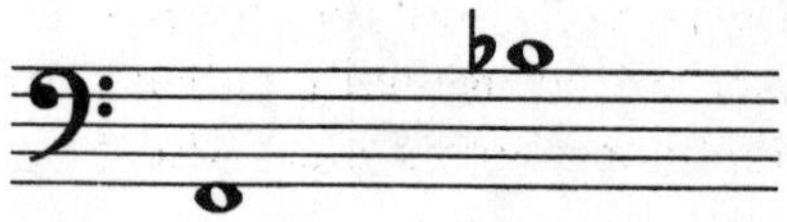

*The substitution of baritone horn or trombone is preferred.
**The substitution of cello is preferred.

The problem of balance will not always be solvable. Obviously, such a combination as flute, trombone, and tuba would not be easy to balance. Since the musical examples are not technically difficult, it is expected that there will be some degree of flexibility within the teams of four musicians, and that each individual student participating might be able to double on another member within his own family of instruments. The combination of flute, trombone and tuba would be a far less serious problem if the trombonist could double on French horn, and the tuba player could play baritone horn.

With three B flat clarinetists in the ensemble, one could play bass clarinet.

Below are listed some combinations which could be used, in addition to the ideal combinations such as violin-viola-cello, oboe-clarinet-bassoon, trumpet-horn-baritone, and alto-tenor-baritone saxophones.

TABLE 2

Treble	Tenor	Bass
flute	French horn	bass clarinet
clarinet	clarinet	trombone
trumpet	alto saxophone	cello
violin	violin	baritone saxophone
oboe	French horn	baritone horn
flute	English horn	string bass (cello)
viola	tenor saxophone	bassoon

There are more than six hundred possible combinations of instruments which may be used. Again, some players will have to transpose, since all parts are written in concert pitch. This should not present a serious obstacle for the experienced music student though, as the examples make only slight technical demands on the performers. (However, because of the unusual technical difficulties which the trombone has in playing rapidly moving passages, some of the exercises will be awkward for most trombonists. In this case, if another instrument can be found for the bass part, the ensemble will gain in facility.) In addition, most instrumentalists must learn to transpose in preparation for the performance of orchestral literature unless they play a concert pitch instrument, and the ability to transpose is an absolute necessity for the conductor. Therefore, the student in the conducting class who is thrust into a situation in which he must transpose is broadening his musicianship as an instrumentalist and as a conductor. Again, the examples are so technically simple that they require little virtuosity on the part of the player.

Transpositional techniques developed through frequent exposure to these exercises in concert pitch can be immediately utilized by clarinet, trumpet, French horn and saxophone players who must be able to transpose concert pitch parts. Violists, cellists, bassoonists, trombonists and baritone horn players will find the technique of reading treble clef parts of great practical value. Bass clarinetists are occasionally called upon to transpose from a concert pitch bass clef part, and baritone saxophone players must also be able to make the necessary transposition from a bass clef part.

Certainly one of the most important daily assignments for the conducting class which uses these materials would be to have each student master at least two of the parts on his instrument (or instruments) as the exercises are assigned.

USING THE MATERIALS

With regards to the procedure for applying these materials in the class, this will depend on various factors of the individual class, i.e., number of students and teams within the class, talent and background of the students enrolled, the amount of time required for each to meet outside of class, etc.

If the class contains enough students for more than one team, as almost all conducting classes do, it might be advisable to vary the class procedure from day to day. One class period could be devoted to the performance of one instrumental team (possibly rotating its members), while all other students take brief turns on the podium to encounter the conducting problem for that day.

Another class meeting could be held in more than one room, with a conducting team in each room, and the instructor and one or more of the most advanced students moving from room to room to observe and to make suggestions.

DOUBLING OF THE VOICES

The instructor of the conducting class should be cautioned against indiscriminate doubling of any of the three voices of the ensemble. Octave doubling of the treble line by a competent violinist or flutist is most desirable, although a weak violinist or flutist will add greatly to the musical problems of the student conductor.

Doubling of the tenor voice by two of the same instruments (e.g., two clarinets, two or more violins or violas) is possible. Such doubling as saxophone, bassoon, and viola on the tenor part is not advisable.

Ideal bass doubling would be string bass below any other bass instrument except tuba. The tuba is the most unwieldly instrument for this ensemble, because of the tessitura assigned to the bass part—a bit high for comfortable tuba playing. Bassoon or cello doubling at the octave with another bass instrument is also possible where the range permits. A lighter unison doubling combination such as bassoon-cello, more than one cello, or bassoon-bass clarinet would also be acceptable.

Intonation, blending, and balance are the factors to be considered in such a decision.

It is advisable that the student conductor be subjected to the constructive criticism of all members of the class in addition to that of the instructor. If one member of the ensemble feels he was not given a convincing cue, for example, or that the down-beat was vague, he should point that out to the conductor.

The instructor is also encouraged to create his own exercises for a given problem. It is not necessary, particularly during the first few days of a conducting class, or when a new subject such as cuing comes up in class, to rely on music, or even students with instruments. Such basic conducting problems as attacks, releases, crescendos, diminuendos, cuing, and unusual meter patterns can be introduced to the student without music or instruments as those problems appear. For example, $\frac{5}{4}$ time could be practiced with the use of rhythmic vocal sounds—words, commands, numbers or even nonsense syllables—enabling the student to approach $\frac{5}{4}$ time at least temporarily without worrying about too many musical problems.

Chapter 8

Baton Technique

What should be the role, or function, of good baton technique or conducting technique? An outstanding orchestral musician who has spent more than twenty years in one of America's leading orchestras defined this function as "providing the meter against which I play." Other orchestral musicians have described this function as "providing the rhythmic impulse to which the orchestra members relate." No matter in which terms this function is expressed—perhaps differently by each musician—it can only mean that the conductor provides certain signals at a given time to which the orchestra members respond. A conductor whose signals are clear and uncomplicated will communicate more clearly to the musicians in less time.

Certainly with an amateur orchestra, a simple conducting style will be most understandable. Perhaps the conductor of an orchestra of the best professional musicians can afford the luxury of an extravagant and theatrical baton technique, but with a lesser orchestra, such a technique can only slow the learning process and endanger the overall performance. It is interesting to note that orchestral musicians in the United States speak most fondly of Leopold Stokowski and Eugene Ormandy, both noted for their economical and clear conducting styles.

It is important that the student conductor learn to conduct even the most elementary patterns with utmost clarity, and that he not be encouraged to attempt more difficult works involving complicated patterns and other hand gestures until his basic meter patterns are clear and secure. An inherent danger in any beginning conducting class is the premature use of difficult works—those involving conducting problems beyond the capabilities of the students. Frequently the student is expected to work with a symphonic movement from the classical period (Beethoven, Schubert) before he has had opportunity to develop clear basic conducting patterns, and before he has had opportunity to develop confidence in the execution of such fundamentals as attacks, cues, dynamic changes, etc.

This text does not advocate any one approach to the design of the basic meter patterns involved in baton technique. One must recognize that there are many successful conductors with many different styles of baton technique. It is also true, however, that there are many conductors who do not conduct in a style which is easy to follow—sometimes due to such a weakness as an "illegible" 4/4 pattern. If the student conductor has a clear concept of what the orchestral musician is looking for in conducting, he will be better able to communicate with that musician.

THE BASIC CONDUCTING PATTERNS

The baton patterns for the basic meters of one, two, three and four beats per measure as recommended in this text are quite standard.

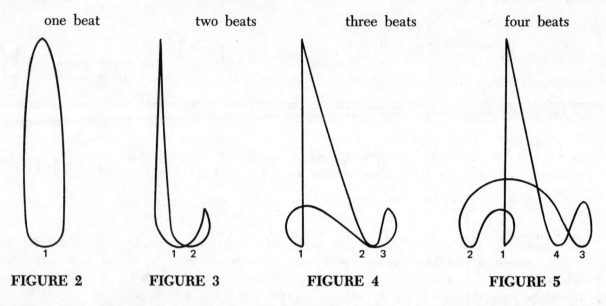

one beat	two beats	three beats	four beats
FIGURE 2	FIGURE 3	FIGURE 4	FIGURE 5

Note that each beat moves initially in a downward direction, including the final beat of each pattern (for example, the second beat in the two beat pattern). This provides a plane, or horizontal line to which each beat gesture moves. It is the arrival of the beat at this plane or line which signifies the initial moment of each beat, and the time involved in moving to the plane for the next beat represents the continuation of the duration of the first beat. For example, if we counted a slow three beats per measure and let the number "one" represent the initial moment of beat one, and the syllables "ee-and-a" represent the time between the beginning of beat one and the beginning of beat two, it would be illustrated as follows:

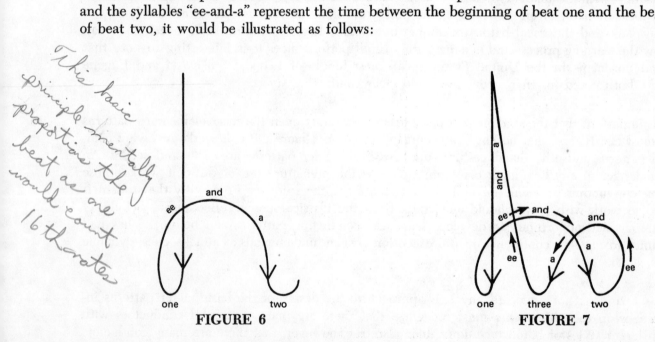

FIGURE 6   FIGURE 7

This basic principle mentally proportions the beat as one would count 16th notes

The same principal would apply in moving from beats two to three, and again in returning from beat three to beat one (Figure 7).

We can reasonably conclude from this observation that the pattern of three beats per measure, as well as all of the other patterns—one, two, and four beats per measure—will have considerable stress in the movement immediately before the plane in each beat. The degree of stress will of course be influenced by the character of the music—a slow passage will require less stress in moving to the plane than a fast, or heavy passage.

THE FIRST BEAT PREPARATION AND THE DOWNBEAT

The gesture which prepares the musicians for a precise entrance signaling the exact moment for a breath, raised mallet, or any other physical preparation necessary before the attack, is called the *preparatory beat*. Let us consider the preparation for the first beat of any measure.

The preparatory beat is somewhat similar to the upbeat, or final beat of an imaginary measure which might have preceded the downbeat. All conducting patterns will have as their final beat the movement upward to the beginning position. In the case of the two beat pattern

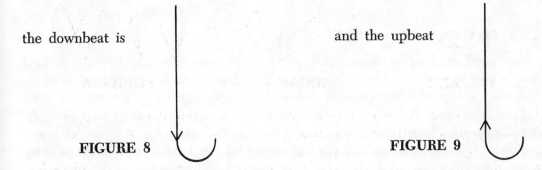

the downbeat is **FIGURE 8**   and the upbeat **FIGURE 9**

the upbeat being approximately the reverse of the downbeat. From this we derive our preparatory beat, which is much like the upbeat.

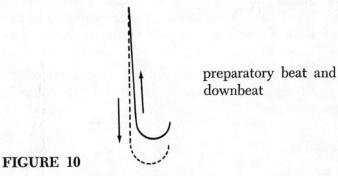

preparatory beat and downbeat

FIGURE 10

As to the application of the preparatory beat, we can relate it to the beginning of a foot-race —another event which must begin with split-second timing. In this instance there are three commands:

1. get ready
2. set
3. go

Or, in a more organized track meet:

1. take your marks
2. get set
3. starting gun fires

In a musical setting, we have the following comparisons:

1. ready — conductor in position, baton raised, ready for the preparatory beat, musicians with instruments in position are alert.
2. set — preparatory beat, players breathe or move bows or mallets to the exact position for the attack.
3. go — attack.

A student conductor certainly need not experience a lack of opportunity to practice his preparatory beat and attack, since this can be done with one or more musicians (or even non-musicians) using words such as "go," "stop," or "hey," without the necessity of relying on printed music. (Consider also the preparation for an attack—"rah"—used by a cheerleader—a valid comparison.) This should be practiced as a rhythmic problem. Dozens of problems can be improvised varying the conducting pattern, the tempo, and the dynamic level. Using just $\frac{2}{4}$, $\frac{3}{4}$, and $\frac{4}{4}$ time, with three dynamic levels and three tempi, we already have twenty-seven different problems for the practice of the preparatory beat and attack, using as yet only the first beat attack.

METER AND THE CONDUCTING PATTERNS

A conductor must have an absolute command of rhythm. He must possess a rhythmic security equal to or superior to that of any member of his ensemble. Indeed, even the interpretation of the meter signatures of some compositions requires a good deal of understanding of the basic structure of rhythm.

The student of conducting should establish as one of his primary goals the mastery of rhythm to the best of his ability. Only if a musician can read with accuracy rhythmic patterns of considerable complexity is he prepared to undertake the responsibility of conducting an ensemble—even of younger school-age children.

At the conclusion of this chapter will be found ten relatively complex patterns which can be used to test the students' rhythmic aptitude. If a student has undue difficulties with the examples —that is, if he cannot read the entire page after a few minutes on each exercise—he is most likely in need of a great deal of rhythmic training as a prerequisite to the study of instrumental conducting.

The following pages will attempt to present the basic conducting patterns in the most logical rhythmic manner possible, so that the student will be able to relate his conducting patterns to his knowledge of meter signatures.

MEASURING TIME

In order to keep track of time, whether in great or minute amounts, man has found it necessary to use various measuring units, i.e., centuries, days, seconds, milliseconds, etc. Music, being a "time-art" as it is, likewise requires the use of units of measurement.

The earliest developments in music—especially in rhythm—cannot be considered apart from their association with the early developments in dance. Consequently the simplest and most logical unit of musical measurement is the step—or beat. We also have an accurate means of establishing the tempo of the beat—by relating to a given number of beats per minute as indicated on a metronome, although the essence of musicality is flexibility within a given tempo.

Using the beat as our basic unit of measurement we can also be quite exact in our organization of the beat into groups of beats, or measures, and thus into larger units—phrases—and ultimately into full compositions. We can also divide and sub-divide the beat into micro units, so that a beat of approximately one second, for example, can easily be divided into sixteen parts.

It is the latter aspect of our organization of beats which is most frequently not understood by music students. A conductor must have a very clear understanding of the nature of the beat and its various divisions. A comprehensive course in rhythmic reading should certainly clarify this matter for the music student. Although it is not the purpose of this workbook to present such a course, a brief review of certain basic rhythmic tenets is in order before we present the conducting patterns.

THE BEAT AND ITS DIVISIONS

1. The beat is our basic unit of measurement.
2. Almost all of our music consists of beats of either two or three parts. (In the case of rapid $\frac{5}{8}$ time, a two and a three part beat occur in each measure.)
3. A clear understanding of the nature of the beat in any composition is essential in order to understand that composition.

TABLE 3

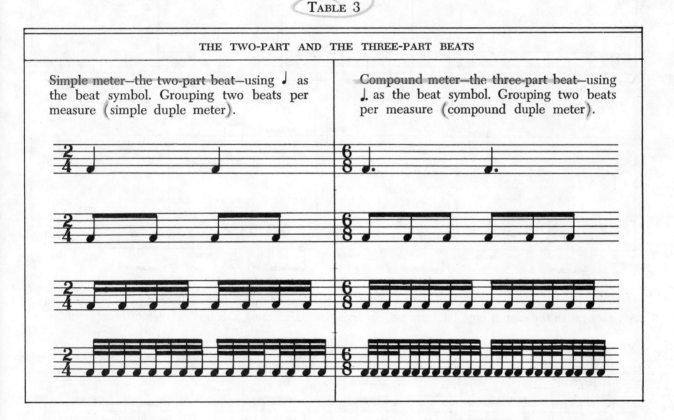

THE TWO-PART AND THE THREE-PART BEATS

Simple meter—the two-part beat—using ♩ as the beat symbol. Grouping two beats per measure (simple duple meter).

Compound meter—the three-part beat—using ♩. as the beat symbol. Grouping two beats per measure (compound duple meter).

Using variations on the above patterns, we can construct measures which are quite complex, such as the following.

EXAMPLE 23 Simple meter

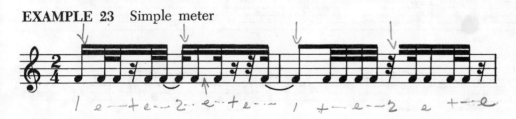

EXAMPLE 24   Compound meter

A mastery of the above rhythmic examples requires a recognition of the complexity of each problem in relation to the basic divisions and subdivisions of the simple and compound beats as shown in B, C, and D of Table 3. The following three examples contain problems typical of those which confront the conductor, and which must be clearly understood before he can appear before his ensemble with such problems.

EXAMPLE 25

In the above example, the conductor must conduct a beat of three parts, followed by two beats of two parts each, with the eighth note background, or division, maintaining a consistent value throughout.

EXAMPLE 26

In the preceding example, the meter change in measure (3) requires a change in the length of the beat, to accommodate an additional eighth note. The value of the background beat, or the beat division unit—in this case the eighth note—remains constant. Contrarily, the meter change in measure (9) necessitates a consistent beat length $\;\downarrow.=\downarrow\;$ while the value of the unit of division—the eighth note of $\frac{6}{8}$ time—becomes faster than the eighth note of $\frac{2}{4}$ time.

EXAMPLE 27 Brahms: 2nd Symphony in D, op. 73. 1st movement m.254-m.257

In the above example the wind instruments play simple patterns which can easily relate to the $\frac{3}{4}$ (simple triple) meter signature. The string parts, on the other hand, suggest a $\frac{6}{8}$ (compound duple) meter signature. The conductor must be able to bring forth from the orchestra on these parts a feeling of $\frac{6}{8}$ time, while retaining the $\frac{3}{4}$ meter among the musicians who are playing the more obvious $\frac{3}{4}$ patterns. Here again, the problem is one of understanding the beat and its division into two or three parts.

It should be quite clear that the student or conductor who does not have a secure rhythmic background will have difficulties with the preceding problems, and that a student with a sound background in rhythmic analysis and rhythmic reading, including an understanding of the nature of the beat division in simple and compound meter, will have little difficulty with the same problems.

The reader will have observed that in the discussion of baton patterns at the opening of this chapter, no reference was made to meter signatures. The purpose of this omission was to introduce the conducting patterns through an awareness of the beat only, with no reference to the background, or division of the beat. After the student has developed his baton technique on the four most common patterns—one, two, three and four beats per measure—and if he clearly understands the rhythmic implications of the divided beat—both simple and compound—he can then more thoroughly develop his ability to interpret and conduct the various meter signatures. This will apply to both simple and compound meters and it will apply particularly to his study of the divided beat patterns, i.e., conducting $\frac{4}{4}$ as slow $\frac{8}{8}$ time, or conducting $\frac{6}{8}$ as six beats per measure, etc., (chap. 12) and to meters involving asymmetrical beats (chap. 13).

The following tables (Tables 4 and 5) contain the basic conducting patterns of one, two, three, and four beats per measure, and the various meter signatures which relate to those patterns. In

TABLE 4

BASIC PATTERN		SIMPLE METER SIGNATURES
	One beat per measure	$\frac{1}{4}$ ♩ or
		$\frac{1}{8}$ ♪ or
		*$\frac{1}{2}$ 𝅗𝅥 or
	Two beats per measure	$\frac{2}{4}$ ♩ ♩ or
		$\frac{2}{8}$ ♪ ♪ or
		¢ $\frac{2}{2}$ 𝅗𝅥 𝅗𝅥 or
		*$\frac{2}{16}$ ♬ ♬ or
	Three beats per measure	$\frac{3}{4}$ ♩ ♩ ♩ or
		$\frac{3}{8}$ ♪ ♪ ♪ or
		$\frac{3}{2}$ 𝅗𝅥 𝅗𝅥 𝅗𝅥 or
		*$\frac{3}{16}$ ♬ ♬ ♬ or
	Four beats per measure	$\frac{4}{4}$ ♩ ♩ ♩ ♩ or
		$\frac{4}{8}$ ♪ ♪ ♪ ♪ or
		$\frac{4}{2}$ 𝅗𝅥 𝅗𝅥 𝅗𝅥 𝅗𝅥 or
		*$\frac{4}{16}$ ♬ ♬ ♬ ♬ or

* Rarely encountered signatures.

Table 4 the four patterns are shown in relation to the simple (two-part beat) meter signatures, and in Table 5 the same four conducting patterns are shown in relation to the compound (three-part beat) patterns.

TABLE 5

BASIC CONDUCTING PATTERNS AND RELATED COMPOUND METER SIGNATURES	
BASIC PATTERN	**COMPOUND METER SIGNATURES**
One beat per measure	$\frac{3}{8}$ or $\frac{3}{4}$ or *$\frac{3}{16}$ or
Two beats per measure	$\frac{6}{8}$ or $\frac{6}{4}$ or *$\frac{6}{16}$ or
Three beats per measure	$\frac{9}{8}$ or $\frac{9}{4}$ or *$\frac{9}{16}$ or
Four beats per measure	$\frac{12}{8}$ or $\frac{12}{4}$ or *$\frac{12}{16}$ or

* Rarely encountered signatures.

The preceding tables should be carefully studied, analyzed, and discussed, particularly from the standpoint of the relationship of any one of the four conducting patterns to its respective meter signatures. The student should be aware of the relationship between $\frac{3}{4}, \frac{3}{8}, \frac{3}{2}$, and $\frac{3}{16}$ time, and how these patterns are dissimilar to $\frac{9}{8}, \frac{9}{4}$, and $\frac{9}{16}$ time. At the same time he should know that all of the aforementioned meters make use of the same three-beat conducting pattern.

The following examples—very elementary in nature—can be used with a few or all performing members of the class, and since they are all in unison or octaves, the instrumentation or doubling which is used by the performers is of little consequence. The purpose of the exercises is to allow each student to get the feel of conducting one, two, three, and four beats per measure with both simple and compound meter backgrounds. It is also desirable that the instructor invent other such exercises and that he encourage each student through homework assignments to do likewise. This particular aspect of the conductor's training should not be overlooked, since he must learn to conduct patterns which relate to the exact value of the beat and background beat. Due to the simplicity of the following exercises, the student has an opportunity to concentrate on this aspect of his beat, and to become aware of the feeling of the background beat with both simple and compound meter. Again, this is one of the most important aspects in the training of a conductor, and no amount of time thus spent will be wasted.

SECTION A

Ten Exercises for the Development of Basic Conducting Patterns

INTRODUCTORY SUGGESTIONS

1. Each exercise may be repeated as many times as the instructor deems necessary for the individual student.
2. It is recommended, particularly when students who are rhythmically insecure are conducting, that a snare drum (and/or other percussion, if available) be added to the ensemble to bring out the background beat.
3. The instructor should determine the dynamic level and tempo of each exercise to be used by the student.

EXERCISE A-1. Simple duple

EXERCISE A-2. Simple triple

EXERCISE A-3. Simple quadruple

EXERCISE A-4. Simple single

(one beat per measure)

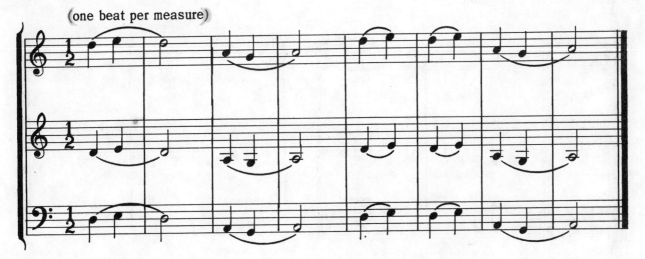

EXERCISE A-5. Simple triple

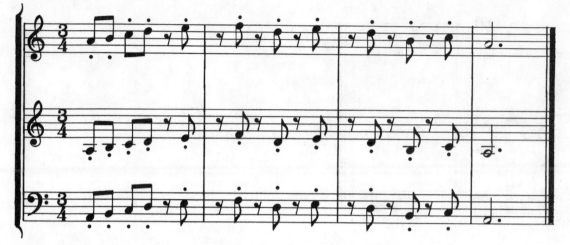

EXERCISE A-6. Compound duple

EXERCISE A-7. Compound triple

EXERCISE A-8. Compound single

EXERCISE A-9. Compound triple

EXERCISE A-10. Compound quadruple

SECTION B

Ten Rhythmic Reading Exercises for Testing the Student's Rhythmic Preparedness.
(not to be conducted)

EXERCISE A-11. Simple duple

EXERCISE A-12. Simple duple

EXERCISE A-13. Simple triple

Slowly – in three

EXERCISE A-14. Simple quadruple

EXERCISE A-15. Simple triple

Moderately — in three

EXERCISE A-16. Simple duple

Slowly — in two

EXERCISE A-17. Compound triple

Allegro molto — in three

EXERCISE A-18. Compound duple

Slowly in 2

EXERCISE A-19. Compound single

Fast

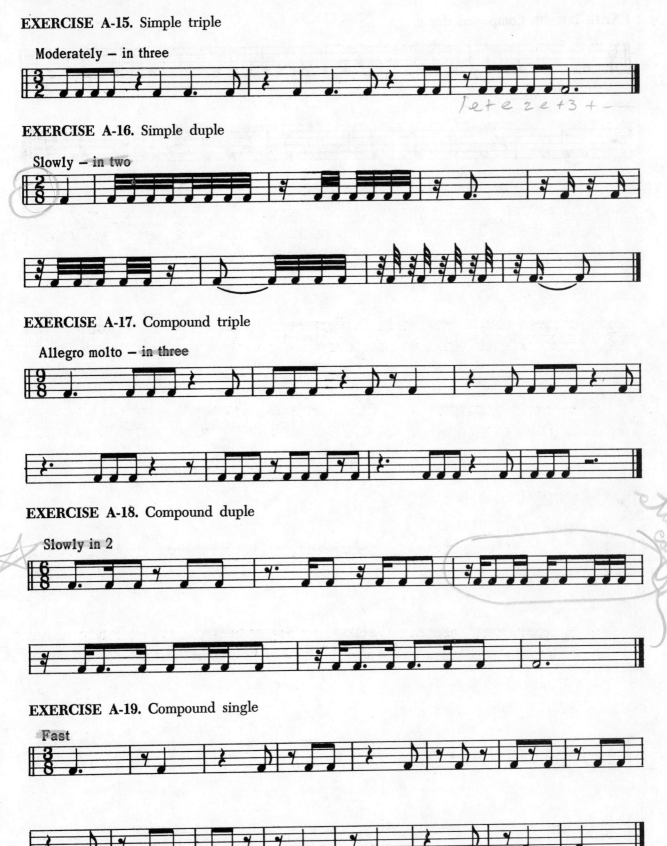

EXERCISE 20. Compound duple

Chapter 9

Attacks and Releases

INTRODUCTORY SUGGESTIONS

1. The dynamic level indicated for each example may be altered with each use of the example. The instructor must of course make clear to the student which dynamic level is to be produced, and he must see that the amplitude of the student's conducting pattern corresponds to that dynamic level.
2. The style of the release, or cut-off, should be consistent with the musical markings of the example.
3. Rests are generally not conducted—especially longer rests. If, however, the beginning student finds it helpful to continue his pattern throughout a rest, a greatly reduced pattern should be used during the rest. Conducting through long silences in a performance is most unprofessional, and is unnecessary.
4. Additional exercises which make use of the same attack problems can be improvised, using scale or arpeggio patterns, or chords, or even vocal sounds, such as "hey," "and one," etc.
5. Exercises B-31 through B-50—off-the-beat attacks—require a full count preparatory beat. If the entrance is on the second half of beat four, for example, the preparatory beat would occupy beat three.
6. Notice the staggered releases in Exercises B-4, B-12, B-15, B-22, and B-23.
7. Many of the exercises in this chapter may be edited in pencil to incorporate problems of the succeeding chapters, thus serving as supplementary material.
8. Every initial attack should be preceded by several seconds of silence. This will make musicians more alert, and it will produce the necessary atmosphere of concentration for the beginning of the musical exercise.
9. *Careful attention should be given to such musical fundamentals as tone quality, intonation, rhythmic ensemble, balance, articulation, bowing, and interpretation.* This is the responsibility of both the student conductor and the conducting instructor.
10. Dotted slur lines indicate optional bowing slur lines for strings.

EXERCISE B-1   **EXERCISE B-2.** Simple duple

EXERCISE B-3. Simple triple

EXERCISE B-4. Simple quadruple. The release of the first fermata and the downbeat for the second measure should occur simultaneously—a single gesture.

EXERCISE B-5. Compound quadruple

EXERCISE B-6

EXERCISE B-7. Compound quadruple

Poco adagio

EXERCISE B-8. Simple quadruple

Andante

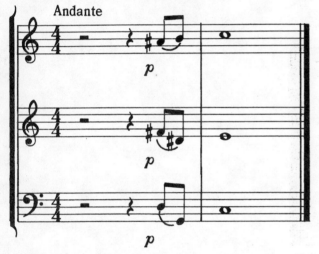

EXERCISE B-9. Simple quadruple

Allegro non troppo

EXERCISE B-10. Simple quadruple

Alla marcia

EXERCISE B-11. Compound quadruple

EXERCISE B-12. Simple quadruple

EXERCISE B-13. Simple quadruple

EXERCISE B-14. Compound quadruple

Leggiero e staccato

EXERCISE B-15. Simple quadruple

Adagio ma non troppo

EXERCISE B-16. Simple quadruple

Marcato

EXERCISE B-17. Simple triple

Sostenuto

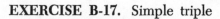

EXERCISE B-18. Compound triple

Sostenuto

EXERCISE B-19. Simple triple

Moderato

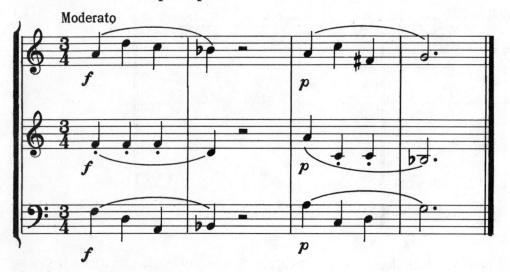

EXERCISE B-20. Compound single

Vivo

EXERCISE B-21. Compound triple

EXERCISE B-22. Simple triple

EXERCISE B-23. Simple triple. Releases in the treble and tenor parts should occur with the downbeat of the following measures.

EXERCISE B-24. Simple quadruple

EXERCISE B-25. Simple triple

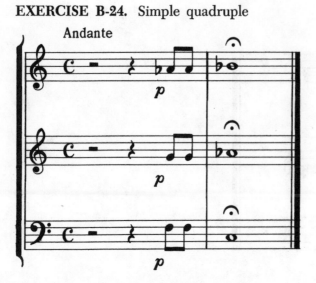

EXERCISE B-26. Compound triple

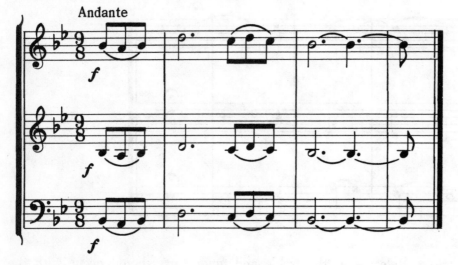

EXERCISE B-27. Simple triple

EXERCISE B-28. Compound duple

Adagietto

EXERCISE B-29. Compound duple

Poco lento

EXERCISE B-30. Compound triple

Agitato

EXERCISE B-31. Simple duple

Allegretto

EXERCISE B-32. Simple quadruple

Allegro

EXERCISE B-33. Simple triple

Laendler

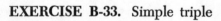

EXERCISE B-34. Simple quadruple

Allegro molto e staccato

EXERCISE B-35. Simple duple

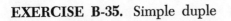

Presto

EXERCISE B-36. Simple triple

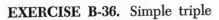

Andante e legato

EXERCISE B-37. Simple triple

Poco vivo

EXERCISE B-38. Simple quadruple

Larghetto

EXERCISE B-39. Simple quadruple

Moderato

EXERCISE B-40. Simple quadruple

EXERCISE B-41. Simple duple

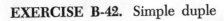

EXERCISE B-42. Simple duple

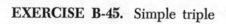

EXERCISE B-43. Simple duple

Marcato

EXERCISE B-44. Compound duple

Allegro

EXERCISE B-45. Simple triple

Langsam

EXERCISE B-46. Simple quadruple

Ritmico

EXERCISE B-47. Compound single

Vivace

EXERCISE B-48. Compound triple

Con moto

EXERCISE B-49. Compound quadruple

Marcato

EXERCISE B-50. Simple quadruple

Marcato

Possible test question

Chapter 10

Crescendo and Diminuendo

INTRODUCTORY SUGGESTIONS

1. Crescendo and diminuendo should be practiced using both the left hand gesture (raising and lowering) and the change of beat size in the right hand. Each technique should first be developed individually before the student attempts both methods. Complete independence of each hand is necessary.
2. The student should practice without music—written or live—until he is able to conduct smoothly any crescendo-diminuendo problem which he devises for himself, e.g., one measure of crescendo and one measure of diminuendo in four-four time. Several such examples are included below, which should suggest to the student additional conducting problems of the same nature. The instructor can also assign problems for the student to master outside of class.
3. Although emphasis in this chapter is on gradual dynamic change, both the instructor and student should strive for clarity in attacks and releases as was stressed in the preceding chapter.

CRESCENDO-DIMINUENDO PROBLEMS FOR PRACTICE:

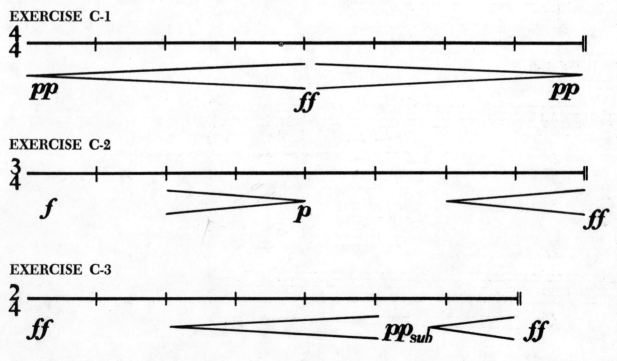

EXERCISE C-1

EXERCISE C-2

EXERCISE C-3

EXERCISE C-4

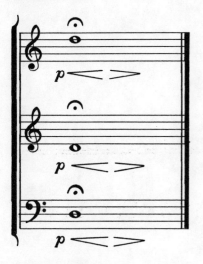

EXERCISE C-5

EXERCISE C-6

EXERCISE C-7

Andante

EXERCISE C-8

Allegretto

EXERCISE C-9

Moderato

EXERCISE C-10

EXERCISE C-11

Poco adagio

EXERCISE C-12

Espressivo

EXERCISE C-13

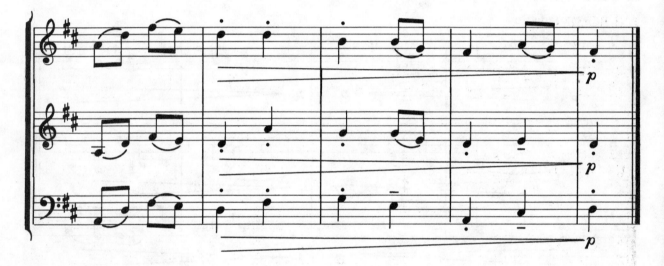

EXERCISE C-14

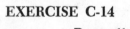

EXERCISE C-15

Langsam

EXERCISE C-16

Schnell

EXERCISE C-17

Moderato e marcato

EXERCISE C-18

Adagio

EXERCISE C-19

Allegro guisto e sempre legato

EXERCISE C-20

Andante con moto

EXERCISE C-21

Con spirito

EXERCISE C-22

Affretando

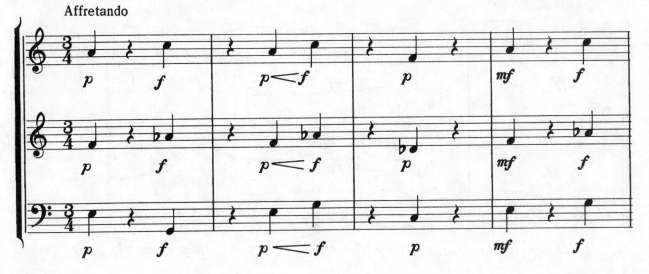

EXERCISE C-23

Andante e rubato

EXERCISE C-24

Allegro ma non troppo

EXERCISE C-25

Andante con moto

EXERCISE C-26

EXERCISE C-27

EXERCISE C-28

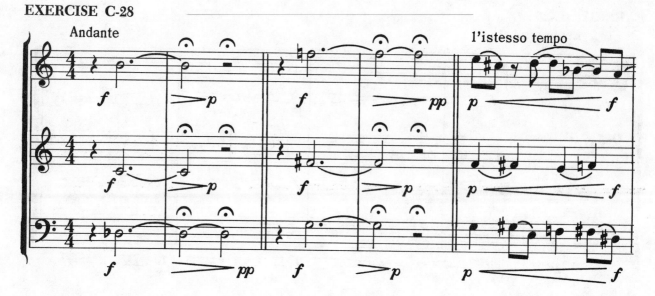

Chapter 11

Cuing

INTRODUCTORY SUGGESTIONS

1. Cuing, like the initial attacks, requires preparation. Although the type of preparation is unlike that of the initial attack, the preparation must come on the beat preceding the entrance, in time to alert the performers. An orchestral player relies perhaps as much on the cue preparation as he does on the cue itself.
2. A variety of cuing methods is advised, using principally the left hand gesture, but also the baton or right hand, the head and eyes, or both hands. This matter is left to the discretion of the instructor.
3. The instructor should suggest a variety of supplementary exercises, using scales, arpeggios, and other fundamental melodic patterns, for the practice of cuing. For example, in $\frac{6}{8}$ time one instrument starts an arpeggiated triplet pattern

etc.

On cue a second instrument starts the same arpeggio or an inversion of it, or an arpeggio in another key.

EXERCISE D-1. Cuing for entrances on beat one in $\frac{4}{4}$

EXERCISE D-2. Cuing for entrances on beat one in $\frac{3}{4}$

EXERCISE D-3. Cuing for entrances on beat one in $\frac{2}{4}$

EXERCISE D-4. Cuing for entrances on beat two in $\frac{3}{4}$

EXERCISE D-5. Cuing for entrances on beat three in $\frac{3}{2}$

Largo

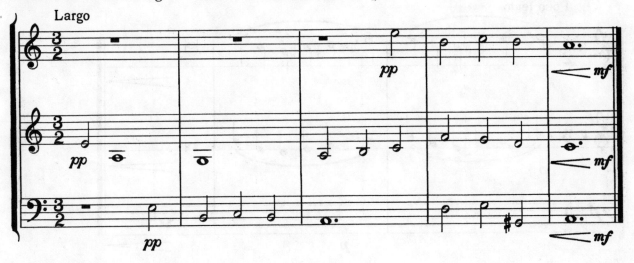

EXERCISE D-6. Cuing for entrances on beat four in $\frac{4}{8}$

Moderato

EXERCISE D-7. Cuing for entrances on beats two and three in $\frac{4}{2}$

EXERCISE D-8. Cuing for entrances on beats one and three in $\frac{4}{4}$

EXERCISE D-9. Cuing for entrances on beat three in $\frac{4}{8}$

Moderato

EXERCISE D-10. Cuing for entrances on beat three in $\frac{3}{4}$

Con moto

EXERCISE D-11.   Cuing for entrances on beats one and three in $\frac{4}{4}$

Allegro

EXERCISE D-12. Cuing for entrances on beat two in $\frac{3}{16}$

EXERCISE D-13. Cuing for entrances on second beat in $\frac{6}{8}$

EXERCISE D-14. Cuing for entrances on beats two and three in ¾

EXERCISE D-15. Cuing for entrances on beat two in 9/8

EXERCISE D-16. Cuing for entrances on all beats in $\frac{12}{8}$

EXERCISE D-17.   Cuing for entrances on beats one and two in $\frac{6}{8}$ (in two)

EXERCISE D-18.   Cuing for entrances on beat one in $\frac{3}{4}$ (in one)

EXERCISE D-19. Cuing for entrances on various beats in $\frac{9}{8}$

EXERCISE D-20. Cuing for entrances before beat one in $\frac{2}{4}$

EXERCISE D-21. Cuing for entrances before beat one in $\frac{3}{4}$

EXERCISE D-22.   Cuing for entrances before beat one in $\frac{4}{4}$

EXERCISE D-23.   Cuing for entrances before beat two in $\frac{2}{4}$

EXERCISE D-24.   Cuing for entrances after beat one in $\frac{3}{4}$

EXERCISE D-25. Cuing for entrances after beat one in $\frac{4}{4}$

Alla marcia

EXERCISE D-26. Cuing for entrances after beat two in $\frac{3}{4}$

Waltz tempo

EXERCISE D-27. Cuing for entrances after beat two in $\frac{4}{4}$

Molto vivace

EXERCISE D-28. Cuing for entrances before and after various beats in $\frac{4}{4}$

EXERCISE D-29. Cuing for entrances after beats one and two in $\frac{9}{8}$ (in three)

Pesante

EXERCISE D-30. Cuing for entrances after various beats in $\frac{12}{8}$

EXERCISE D-31. Cuing for entrances after second beat in $\frac{6}{8}$

EXERCISE D-32. Cuing for entrances after beats one and two in $\frac{6}{4}$

EXERCISE D-33. Cuing for entrances before, on and after the beat in $\frac{3}{8}$

EXERCISE D-34. Cuing for entrances on and after all beats in $\frac{4}{2}$. The caesura at the beginning of the fourth measure may be followed by a small preparatory beat to insure a precise re-entry of the bass.

EXERCISE D-35.   Cuing for entrances after various beats in $\frac{9}{8}$

EXERCISE D-36.   Cuing for entrances after beats one and two in $\frac{6}{8}$

EXERCISE D-37. Cuing for entrances on, before, and after the beat in $\frac{2}{8}$. Note the fermata, which necessitates the cut-off gesture within the measure, similar to an extra beat. There should be no hesitation following the fermata. In fact, the fermata release should serve as preparation for beat two.

EXERCISE D-38. Cuing for entrances before and after each beat in $\frac{9}{4}$. Careful attention must be given to the entrances, as they are not all rhythmically consistent.

EXERCISE D-39.   Cuing for entrances before and after all beats in $\frac{12}{8}$

EXERCISE D-40. Cuing for entrances on, before and after various beats in $\frac{9}{8}$

Chapter 12

Divided Meters

INTRODUCTORY SUGGESTIONS

1. The divided beat concept in this chapter includes the division of both the simple (two-part) beat and the compound (three-part) beat. Therefore, we deal with a two *and* a three part division of each beat of a one, two, three or a four beat measure. For example, a two beat measure can be divided into four beats, as in the case of two simple beats, and six beats, as in the case of two compound beats such as $\frac{6}{8}$.
2. Tables 6 and 7 at the beginning of this chapter should be studied and discussed in great detail. The student should develop considerable skill in conducting the divided beat patterns by working with very basic examples such as scales and other melodic patterns.
3. Exercises E-1 through E-13 involve the division of simple beats. Exercises E-14 through E-27 involve the division of compound beats.
4. Many exercises from preceding chapters may be used for practicing the divided beat patterns by using a slower tempo than indicated in those exercises.
5. The student should be aware that the use of the divided beat is always based on the question of tempo. When the required tempo is too slow to accomodate comfortably a regular (non-divided) pattern, rhythmic flow will best be maintained by dividing the beat.

DIVIDED SIMPLE METER SIGNATURES

EXERCISE E-1. Divided one

Slowly (in two)

EXERCISE E-2. Divided three

Lento

EXERCISE E-3. Divided three

Grave

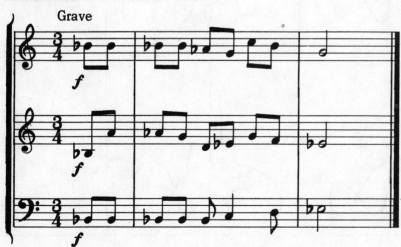

TABLE 6 THE TWO-PART DIVISION OF THE BEAT

	BASIC PATTERN	TWO-PART DIVISION OF BASIC PATTERN	COMMON SIGNATURES
One beat per measure			$\frac{1}{2}$ $\frac{1}{4}$ $\frac{1}{8}$
Two beats per measure			$\frac{2}{8}$ $\frac{2}{4}$ $\frac{2}{2}$
Three beats per measure			$\frac{3}{16}$ $\frac{3}{8}$ $\frac{3}{4}$ $\frac{3}{2}$
Four beats per measure			$\frac{4}{16}$ $\frac{4}{8}$ $\frac{4}{4}$ $\frac{4}{2}$

TABLE 7 THE THREE-PART DIVISION OF THE BEAT

	BASIC PATTERN	THREE PART DIVISION OF BASIC PATTERN	
One beat per measure			$\frac{3}{16}$ $\frac{3}{8}$ $\frac{3}{4}$
Two beats per measure			$\frac{6}{16}$ $\frac{6}{8}$ $\frac{6}{4}$
Three beats per measure			$\frac{9}{16}$ $\frac{9}{8}$ $\frac{9}{4}$
Four beats per measure			$\frac{12}{16}$ $\frac{12}{8}$ $\frac{12}{4}$

EXERCISE E-4. Divided two

EXERCISE E-5. Divided two

EXERCISE E-6. Divided four

EXERCISE E-7. Divided three

EXERCISE E-8. Divided four

EXERCISE E-9. Divided two

EXERCISE E-10. Divided one

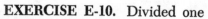

EXERCISE E-11. Divided two

Deliberately

EXERCISE E-12. Divided two

Adagio ma non troppo

EXERCISE E-13. Divided four

Espressivo

DIVIDED COMPOUND METER SIGNATURES

EXERCISE E-14. Divided two (six beats per measure)

EXERCISE E-15. Divided two (six beats per measure)

EXERCISE E-16. Divided one

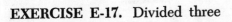

EXERCISE E-17. Divided three

EXERCISE E-18. Divided three

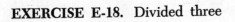

EXERCISE E-19. Divided two

Deciso

EXERCISE E-20. Divided two

Amabile

EXERCISE E-21. Divided four

Grazia

EXERCISE E-22. Divided two

Moderato

EXERCISE E-23. Divided two

Lento

EXERCISE E-24. Divided three

EXERCISE E-25. Divided three

EXERCISE E-26. Divided two

Marcato

EXERCISE E-27. Divided two

Adagio assai

ADDITIONAL DIVIDED SIMPLE METER SIGNATURES

The following exercise (Ex. E-28), which is a reduction for the three-part ensemble of the opening measures of Mozart's *Overture to the Magic Flute,* may be conducted in any one of several ways:
1. The sixteenth note and the following half note may each receive a separate beat.
2. The sixteenth note may be the last half of the second of *two* eighth note preparatory beats. This method is advantageous in that it fixes a very definite tempo for the entrance of the sixteenth.
3. The sixteenth note may be part of a quarter note preparatory beat preceding the half note. This method necessitates a very careful ensemble response from each player.
4. The sixteenth may be interpreted as an anticipation of the downbeat for the half note. In this case, the sixteenth is interpreted as a very short note, and appears close to the half note.

EXERCISE E-28. Divided four

The following exercise should be conducted in two ways—(1) interpreting the fermata releases or cut-offs as the gesture for entrance after the sixteenth rests, and (2) delaying after the fermata releases, and using a new gesture for the entrance following the rests.

EXERCISE E-29

EXERCISE E-30. Beethoven: Symphony #1 in C, Op. 21, Finale (The instrumentation has been reduced for the trio.)

Adagio

Allegro molto e vivace

Chapter 13

Unusual Rhythms and Meters

INTRODUCTORY SUGGESTIONS

1. This chapter is divided into five sections. They are:
   a. Meters involving asymmetrical beat groups, but symmetrical beat divisions;
   b. Changing meters, involving asymmetrical beat groups, but symmetrical beat divisions;
   c. Meters involving asymmetrical beat divisions;
   d. Changing meters, involving asymmetrical beat divisions;
   e. Polyrhythms and polymeters.
2. In an effort to thoroughly understand the exercises which follow, the reader is referred to the discussion of the organization of the beat and its simple or compound divisions, found in chapter eight. The student should be aware that it is the use of asymmetrical beat divisions, such as those found in sections C and D of this chapter, which will create the greatest obstacle for most students. Unless the student has a command of rhythm which enables him to skillfully handle such asymmetrical patterns, his competence as a musician, and especially as a conductor, will be seriously limited.
3. One important point should be emphasized in dealing with patterns in excess of five beats per measure, such as seven beats, or the asymmetrical grouping of eight or nine beats per measure as in exercise F-3, F-4, F-6 and F-7. These patterns can be simply constructed by using various combinations of the regular (non-divided) beat form and the simple and compound divided beat forms.

For example, using a hypothetical example of $\frac{11}{8}$, we might find the general pattern of rhythm to be

$$\frac{11}{8}$$

We therefore construct our conducting pattern by using three compound (three-part) divided beats, followed by one simple (two-part) divided beat, and our pattern is quite similar to a $\frac{12}{8}$ pattern with beats ten and eleven having the form of the fourth beat (divided) in slow $\frac{4}{4}$ time.

A conducting pattern for $\frac{11}{8}$ time.

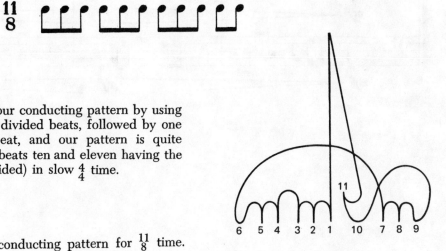

FIGURE 11

133

4. Additional examples of conducting problems involving asymmetrical beat groups and beat divisions can be found in chapters two, three, and four of *The Conductor's Art,* by Warwick Braithwaite, published by John de Graff Inc., 1952. These examples are not for ensemble performance, but provide challenging material for the student conductor to study alone or with one other person.

SECTION A

Meters Involving Asymmetrical Beat Groups, but Symmetrical Beat Divisions

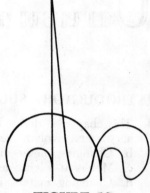

FIGURE 12

EXERCISE F-1

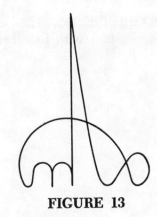

FIGURE 13

EXERCISE F-2

EXERCISE F-3. The seven beat pattern shown in Figure 14, or a pattern of three beats alternating with four beats may be used.

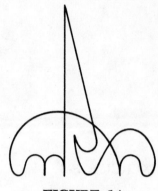

FIGURE 14

EXERCISE F-4. An alternating pattern of four and three beats, or the following pattern of seven may be used.

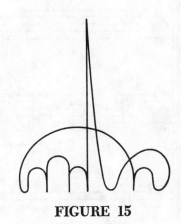

FIGURE 15

EXERCISE F-5

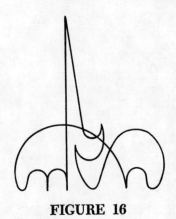

FIGURE 16

EXERCISE F-6. Conducted in eight.

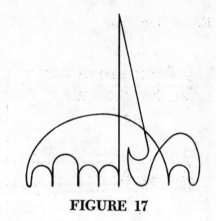

FIGURE 17

EXERCISE F-7

EXERCISE F-8

SECTION B

Changing Meters Involving Asymmetrical Beat Groups, but Symmetrical Beat Divisions

EXERCISE F-9

Con moto

EXERCISE F-10

Allegro assai

EXERCISE F-11

EXERCISE F-12

EXERCISE F-13

EXERCISE F-14

SECTION C

Meters Involving Asymmetrical Beat Divisions

The exercises in both Section C and Section D make use of conducting patterns which follow the general shape of the regular (non-divided) conducting patterns of one, two, three, and four beats per measure, but with considerably altered timing of those beats. The fast $\frac{5}{8}$ meter, for example, is conducted using two beats of different lengths, since one beat has three divisions and the other beat has only two. So in exercise F-15, we use a compound (three-part) beat and a simple (two-part) beat, or a long beat and a short beat in the same measure.

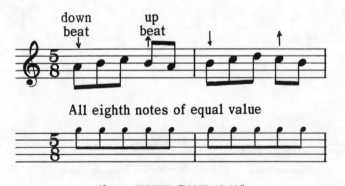

All eighth notes of equal value

(from EXERCISE F-15)

The same principle would apply in the case of fast $\frac{7}{8}$, with two short beats and one long beat, or one short and one long and another short beat, or one long and two short beats, depending on the phrasing demanded by the composer. Each of the three possibilities for $\frac{7}{8}$ time would be conducted with a pattern of three, but with beats of unequal length. The principle would apply to all asymmetrical meters. (Exercises F-15 through F-31.)

EXERCISE F-15

Energico

EXERCISE F-16

Furioso

EXERCISE F-17

Einfach

EXERCISE F-18. Various tempi, as well as other scales (keys) should be employed with this rhythmic pattern.

EXERCISE F-19

Scherzando

EXERCISE F-20

EXERCISE F-21. Conducted in four; the final beat in the last full measure may be divided into three.

EXERCISE F-22. Conducted in four

EXERCISE F-23. Conducted in four

EXERCISE F-24

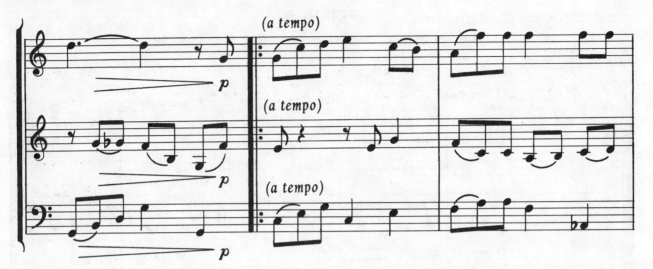

SECTION D
Changing Meters Involving Asymmetrical Beat Divisions

EXERCISE F-25

EXERCISE F-26

EXERCISE F-27 Conducted in alternating two and three

Animato

EXERCISE F-28

EXERCISE F-29.

Moderato

EXERCISE F-30

EXERCISE F-31

SECTION E

Polyrhythms and Polymeters

Suggestions:

1. When polyrhythms occur, one or more voices might contain beats which do not coincide with the pattern which is being conducted, as in the case of triplet quarter notes occupying the entire measure in $\frac{2}{4}$ time. In this case only the first beat of each measure will serve as a beat for all members of the ensemble. The conductor should therefore stress the first beat. The other beat or beats in the measure are consequently de-emphasized—the amount of de-emphasis depending on the tempo or length of the measure. In the case of Ex. F-36, which has measures of short duration, the second beat may be eliminated entirely, with the conductor conducting one beat per measure.

2. As with previous exercises, the student conductor should be advised to practice these exercises with the omission of one part before conducting all three parts together. In Ex. F-34, tenor and bass should first be played together, then treble and tenor together. This enables the conductor and the members of the ensemble to more accurately relate the various parts to each other.

EXERCISE F-32

EXERCISE F-33. This exercise should be conducted in two, with the first beat of each measure emphasized. Since the musician playing the $\frac{3}{4}$ part will need to relate to that first beat, a strong second beat will make the $\frac{3}{4}$ part more difficult.

EXERCISE F-34. The first beat, as in the preceding example, should be emphasized at the expense of the second beat. This exercise should be first rehearsed with one voice omitted.

EXERCISE F-35. Conducted in three, with the first beat receiving extra emphasis.

EXERCISE F-36. Conducted in one. Each player should be allowed to play his part alone to establish a consistent rhythm.

Molto vivace

Bibliography

Acoustics and Tone

CULVER, CHARLES A. *Musical Acoustics*. New York: McGraw-Hill Book Co., 1956.
JOSEPHS, JESS J. *Physics of Musical Sound*. Princeton: D. Van Nostrand Co. Inc., 1967.
LOWERY, H. *Guide to Musical Acoustics*. London: Dennis Dobson, 1956.
OLSEN, HARRY F. *Music, Physics, and Engineering*. New York: Dover Publications, Inc., 1952.
WINCKEL, FRITZ. *Music, Sound and Sensation*. New York: Dover Publications, Inc., 1967.

Articulation and Bowing

GREEN, ELIZABETH A. H. *Orchestral Bowing and Routines*. Ann Arbor: Ann Arbor Press, 1957.
KELLER, HERMANN. *Phrasing and Articulation*. New York: W. W. Norton, 1965.

Conducting

BAMBURGER, CARL. *The Conductor's Art*. New York: McGraw-Hill, 1965.
BOWLES, MICHAEL A. *The Art of Conducting*. New York: Doubleday and Co., 1959.
BOULT, ADRIAN C. *Thoughts on Conducting*. London: Phoenix House Ltd., 1963.
BRAITHWAITE, WARWICK. *The Conductor's Art*. London: Williams and Norgate, 1952.
COX-IFE, WILLIAM. *Elements of Conducting*. New York: John Day Co., 1964.
EARHART, WILL. *The Eloquent Baton*. New York: M. Witmark and Sons, 1946.
GEHRKINS, KARL WILSON. *Essentials in Conducting*. New York: Oliver Ditson Co., 1919.
GREEN, ELIZABETH A. H. *The Modern Conductor*. Englewood Cliffs, N. J.: Prentice-Hall, 1962.
GROSBAYNE, BENJAMIN. *Techniques of Modern Orchestral Conducting*. Cambridge: Harvard University Press, 1956.
HOLMES, MALCOLM H. *Conducting an Amateur Orchestra*. Cambridge: Harvard University Press, 1951.
KENDRIE, FRANK ESTIES. *Handbook on Conducting and Orchestral Routines*. New York: H. W. Gray Co., 1930.
KRUEGER, KARL. *The Way of the Conductor*. New York: Charles Scribner's Sons, 1958.
McELHERAN, BROCK. *Conducting Technique*. London: Oxford University Press, 1966.
RUDOLF, MAX. *The Grammar of Conducting*. New York: G. Schirmer, 1949.
SAMINSKY, LAZARE. *Essentials of Conducting*. London: Dennis Dobson, 1958.
SCHERCHEN, HERMAN. *Handbook of Conducting*. London: Oxford University Press, 1933.
STOESSEL, ALBERT. *Technique of the Baton*. New York: Carl Fischer, 1920.

Contemporary Music

AUSTIN, WILLIAM A. *Music in the Twentieth Century*. New York: W. W. Norton, 1966.
DERI, OTTO. *Exploring Twentieth Century Music*. New York: Holt, Rinehart and Winston, 1968.

Form

CONE, EDWARD T. *Musical Form and Musical Performance*. New York: W. W. Norton, 1968.
DAVIE, CEDRIC THORPE. *Musical Structure and Design*. London: Dennis Dobson, 1953.
ESCHMAN, KARL. *Changing Forms in Modern Music*. Boston: E. C. Schirmer, 1945.
FONTAINE, PAUL. *Basic Formal Structure in Music*. New York: Appleton-Century-Crofts, 1967.
STEIN, ERWIN. *Form and Performance*. New York: Alfred A. Knopf, 1952.
STEIN, LEON. *Anthology of Musical Forms*. Evanston: Summy-Birchard Co., 1962.
————. *Structure and Style*. Evanston: Summy-Birchard Co., 1962.

Intonation

    POTTLE, RALPH. *Tuning the School Band and Orchestra.* Hammond, La.: Southeastern La. State College, 1960.

    STAUFFER, DONALD W. *Intonation Deficiencies of Wind Instruments, in Ensemble.* Washington: Catholic University Press, 1954.

Orchestral Instruments

    Flute

    ROCKSTRO, RICHARD S. *The Flute.* London: Mussica Rara Press, 1967.

    WILKINS, FREDERICK. *The Flutist's Guide.* Elkhart: D & J Artley, 1957.

    Oboe

    BATE, PHILIP, *The Oboe.* New York: W. W. Norton, 1956.

    SPRENKLE, ROBERT, and LEDET, DAVID. *The Art of Oboe Playing.* Evanston: Summy-Birchard, 1961.

    Clarinet

    RENDALL, GEOFFREY. *The Clarinet.* New York: Philosophical Library, 1954.

    STUBBINS, WILLIAM. *The Art of Clarinetistry.* Ann Arbor: Ann Arbor Press, 1965.

    Bassoon

    LANGWILL, LINDESAY GRAHAM. *The Bassoon and Contra-Bassoon.* New York: W. W. Norton, 1965.

    SPENCER, WM. G. *The Art of Bassoon Playing.* Evanston: Summy-Birchard, 1958.

    Saxophone

    TEAL, LARRY. *The Art of Saxophone Playing.* Evanston: Summy-Birchard, 1963.

    Woodwinds

    BAINES, ANTHONY. *Woodwind Instruments and Their History.* London: Faber and Faber, 1957.

    TIMM, EVERETT L. *The Woodwinds.* Boston: Allyn and Bacon, 1964.

    WESTPHAL, FREDERICK. *Guide to Teaching Woodwinds.* Dubuque, Iowa: Wm. C. Brown Publishing Co., 1962.

    Horn

    FARKES, PHILIP. *The Art of French Horn Playing.* Evanston: Summy-Birchard, 1956.

    GREGORY, ROBIN. *The Horn, A Guide to the Modern Instrument.* London: Faber and Faber, 1961.

    Trumpet

    AUTREY, BYRON. *Basic Guide to Trumpet Playing.* Chicago: M. M. Cole Publishing Co., 1963.

    Trombone

    BATE, PHILIP. *The Trumpet and Trombone.* New York: W. W. Norton, 1966.

    Brass

    BARBOUR, J. MURRAY. *Trumpets, Horns and Music.* East Lansing: Michigan State University Press, 1964.

    HUNT, NORMAN. *Guide to Teaching Brass Instruments.* Dubuque, Iowa: Wm. C. Brown Publishing Co., 1968.

    WINTER, JAMES. *The Brass Instruments.* Boston: Allyn & Bacon, 1964.

Rhythm

    STARER, ROBERT. *Rhythmic Training.* New York: MCA Music, 1969.

Index

NOTES

NOTES

NOTES

NOTES

NOTES